LIGHTHOUSES OF AMERICA

LIGHTHOUSES OF AMERICA

Al Mitchell

CHARTWELL
BOOKS, INC.

Published in 2010 by
CHARTWELL BOOKS, INC.
A division of BOOK SALES, INC.
276 Fifth Avenue Suite 206
New York, NY10001
USA

**Copyright © 2010 Regency
House Publishing Limited**
The Red House
84 High Street
Buntingford
Hertfordshire, SG9 9AJ

ISBN-13: 978-0-7858-2707-8
ISBN-10: 0-7858-2707-2

The photographs in this book have, in the
main, been supplied by John Stuart, with
contributions from Rick Polad and Kent
Edwards. These do not include the
following:

Page 19 © Richard Cummins/CORBIS
Page 23 © Atlantide Phototravel/CORBIS
Page 25 © Robert Holmes/CORBIS
Page 38 © Robert Holmes/CORBIS
Page 43 © Phillip James Corwin/CORBIS
Pages 44-45 © Todd Gipstein/CORBIS
Page 47 © Jean Guichard/CORBIS
Pages 96-97 © Tim Tadder/CORBIS
Page 116 © Free Agents/CORBIS
Pages 134-135 © Jeff Albertson/CORBIS
Page 239 © Richard Cummins/CORBIS

Printed in China

CONTENTS

INTRODUCTION

Maritime lights have been in use since before the dawn of civilization. Prehistoric peoples in coastal areas ventured out to sea in small boats, to fish or to trade with nearby communities. But when the weather turned foul, or daylight ran out and they had still not returned, fires would undoubtedly have been lit to call these early mariners home.

The first great cities of the Middle East were usually located along sea coasts or on the banks of major rivers, where fiery beacons, blazing forth from the tops of lofty temples, both guided and attracted trading vessels into harbor. Among the Seven Wonders of the Ancient World was the lighthouse that was completed during the reign of Ptolemy II of Egypt, in about 280 B.C. Believed to have been more than 400-ft tall, it was built on Pharos, an island in the harbor of the Mediterranean city port of Alexandria, where it stood for more than 1,000 years.

The history of the lighthouse in Europe dates least back to the time of Imperial Rome, when the Emperor Claudius ordered a stone tower to be built to guide ships into Rome's key port of Ostia. The ancient Chinese also made use of coastal beacons of one sort or another, as did the maritime peoples of Polynesia and the Pacific.

FIRST AMERICAN LIGHTS

America, for obvious reasons, cannot claim to have an ancient maritime heritage. The first large ships to be seen in American waters were those of European explorers, who arrived in the 15th and 16th centuries. They found America's coastal waters dark and forbidding, and many ships were lost to uncharted reefs and shoals or to low, all but invisible headlands, that reared up unexpectedly from the tides. The weather along America's coasts was quite different from anything European mariners had experienced before, and there were no lights to guide them to safe harbor when gales and hurricanes struck. Many early colonists had no choice but to build their rough shelters along the coastal shores, in the very places where they had been shipwrecked and washed up.

Government-sponsored or privately-funded lighthouses were becoming increasingly common in Europe by the time the British colonies had taken root in North America. England's famous Eddystone Light was built on an offshore rock near Plymouth in 1698, and there were already lesser coastal beacons marking dozens, if not hundreds of harbors throughout the British Isles and continental Europe. But the early colonists, who had crossed the Atlantic in seach of a new life, lacked the resources to establish major maritime lights, at least for the time being.

This would begin to change in 1716, when work was completed on North America's first true lighthouse, located near the entrance to Boston Harbor. No architectural marvel, the rough stone tower on Lighthouse Island – now called Little Brewster Island – a few miles east of Boston, stood only a few dozen feet tall, its crude beacon lit by candles. Despite its shortcomings, it was capable of guiding ships safely into harbor, and the knowledge that it was there attracted a rising tide of maritime commerce to Boston, allowing local merchants to grow wealthy on the profits from imported porcelain, furniture, cloth, and tea.

In spite of Boston's success, other colonial ports were slow to follow her example. The next beacon to appear along the coast of what was now the United States was established by whalers, who in 1746, marked their home port on Nantucket Island with a small light. Other colonial lights would follow at Beavertail in Rhode Island in 1749, New London, Connecticut in 1760, Sandy Hook in New Jersey in 1764, Cape Henlopen in Delaware in 1767, Charleston, South Carolina in 1767, Plymouth, Massachusetts in 1769, Portsmouth, New Hampshire in 1771, and Cape Ann in Massachusetts in 1771.

Following the Revolutionary War and the ratification of the U.S. Constitution in 1789, the nation's fledgling federal government made lighthouses one of its first priorities. President George Washington had barely taken the oath of office before he was urging Congress to pass the

Lighthouse Act, authorizing the building and maintenance of coastal lights. Washington ordered construction of a considerable number of important new lighthouses, such as those at Portland Head (1791) in Maine, Tybee Island (1791) in Georgia, Cape Henry (1792) in Virginia, Bald Head (1796) in North Carolina, and Montauk Point (1797) in New York; many other lighthouses would follow by order of John Adams, Thomas Jefferson, and succeeding presidents.

For many years the United States lighthouse system would be administered by auditors in the U.S. Treasury Department. Such an arrangement made sense for the small government of a new and not particularly wealthy agricultural country. In time, however, it would have a detrimental effect on the quality of the nation's maritime lights, due, in part, to the parsimony of a single government bureaucrat, a man named Stephen Pleasonton. During the War of 1812, Pleasonton was credited with saving a large number of key documents (among them the original copies of the U.S. Constitution and the Declaration of Independence), when invading British troops set fire to the capitol building in Washington. Pleasonton was made Fifth Auditor of the U.S. Treasury by way of a reward, and was given authority over the nation's lighthouses.

As it turned out, Pleasonton took his responsibilities as an auditor very seriously indeed, scrimping on construction materials and labor, paying low salaries to keepers, and opting for inferior lamps and other equipment. Over the years, Pleasonton developed a close working relationship with contractor, Winslow Lewis, a former sea captain, whose estimates were often considerably lower than those of other builders. Because his budgets were so unrealistic, Lewis's inferior stone and brick light towers were often so badly built that they lasted, at best, only a few years. Some were blown over by storms and others were torn down intentionally, for fear they would fall over and kill someone. Even worse, Lewis managed to persuade Pleasonton to

LIGHTHOUSES OF AMERICA

LEFT: Portland Head Light, Maine.

PAGE 10: Block Island Southeast Light, Rhode Island.

LIGHTHOUSES OF AMERICA

utilize a relatively inexpensive lamp-and-reflector optic or lighting system, that he claimed to have invented himself. In fact, Lewis had borrowed the idea from a European inventor, but more important than the question of its origin was the undeniable fact that the Lewis system worked very poorly indeed. His lamp-and-reflector optics produced a light so dim that navigators often ran their ships onto nearby shoals and beaches without ever having seen the beacon at all.

BRIGHTER LIGHTS ON THE HORIZON

While the coast of the United States was languishing in the lighthouse equivalent of the Dark Ages, European shores were becoming very much brighter. During the 1820s, a French mathematician and scientist, Augustin Fresnel (1788–1827), invented a marvelous lifesaving device. Having successfully challenged Isaac Newton's notion, that light consists of a stream of particles, Fresnel was able to develop the theories of the English polymath, Thomas Young (1723–1829), to prove that light moves in waves. Fresnel also reasoned that when light waves enter a dense material, such as glass, they slow down and change direction. Putting his ideas to a practical use, Fresnel designed massive circular lenses, capable of concentrating light into tightly focused beams visible over great distances. Fresnel's lenses were so advanced that they would remain the best available option for more than a century. Manufactured largely in France, they soon became the optic of choice in lighthouses everywhere in the world – everywhere, that is, apart from the United States.

In addition to being extremely effective, Fresnel lenses were also prohibitively expensive. They were ranked according to size and power, from first-order (largest and brightest) down to sixth-order (smallest and least bright), and a large first-order lens could cost more than the tower, the keeper's residence, and the lighthouse property all put together. Not surprisingly, Pleasonton, an accountant, ignored the Fresnel technology, angrily refusing even to discuss the matter. By the time, in the early 1850s, that an exasperated Congress was finally able to prize America's maritime beacons from Pleasonton's tightfisted grasp, Fresnel's polished glass prisms had been standard equipment in European lighthouses for many decades.

Following a report, that proved highly critical of Pleasonton's stewardship, Congress handed responsibility for the nation's ailing coastal lights over to an appointed Lighthouse Board, consisting of scientists and military officers. Almost immediately, the board launched a major construction program, aimed at marking the eastern seaboard, the west coast, and the shores of the Great Lakes, with the best maritime lights available. Old lighthouses were restored or rebuilt and new ones were constructed to fill previously dark stretches of coast. More importantly, shiploads of Fresnel lenses were imported to brighten the lanterns of every lighthouse in America. All this cost millions, but over the years incalculable savings would be made in terms of both lives and safely delivered cargoes.

The Lighthouse Board remained at the helm for nearly 60 years. Then, in 1910, authority over the nation's coastal lights, lightships, buoys, and channel-markers, was vested in the U.S. Bureau of Lighthouses, a civilian agency headed by an appointed commissioner. The bureau was a sizeable organization, consisting of more than 5,000 keepers and other workers. It had its own fleet of 65 large tenders, a far-flung network of supply depots, and even its own news magazine, the *Lighthouse Service Bulletin*; its reign, however, would last for less than 30 years.

In 1939, with the Second World War on the horizon, President Franklin Delano Roosevelt sought to bolster the nation's coastal defenses by strengthening the U.S. Coast Guard. To achieve this, he dissolved the Bureau of Lighthouses, transferring its duties to the Coast Guard. Civilian keepers were now allowed to remain at their posts until they either resigned or retired, when their positions were filled by Coast Guard military personnel. The Coast Guard still maintains the nation's coastal lights and other aids to navigation. Interestingly, it can trace its heritage back to 1789 and the founding of what has come to be called the U.S. Lighthouse Service.

LIFESAVING TOWERS NOW NEED RESCUE

The lighthouse on Sandy Hook, in New Jersey, has stood for more than two centuries – since 1764, in fact – but most light towers have not or will not last that long. There are many threats to lighthouses, and one has historically been war. In the southern United States, in particular, much of the good work done by Lighthouse Board engineers and construction crews during the 1850s had to be repeated after the American Civil War, after the tragic fratricidal conflict had taken its toll. Most of the lighthouses had been neglected and many had been blasted by cannon fire or blown up with charges of gunpowder by either Union or Confederate forces, eager to render them useless to the enemy side.

A far greater threat, however, has been the relentless march of coastal erosion. Lighthouses built during the 19th century were sited at what was believed, at the time, to be safe distances from the water's edge. In many cases, however, a century or more of erosion has brought the shoreline up to the towers' foundations, with waves threatening to engulf their fragile walls. To save these venerable structures from certain destruction, public and private funds have been used to move them to new locations out of harm's way. This was the case with Rhode Island's Block Island Lighthouse in 1993, and with the Highland or Cape Code Lighthouse in 1996. It happened again at Cape Hatteras in 1999, where, in an extraordinary feat of engineering, a 3,000-ton, 200-ft brick tower was loaded onto rails and over a period of weeks was pushed back inch-by-inch to a new location nearly a third of a mile inland.

More than a few have been less fortunate, however. Last-minute attempts to save the historic Cape St. George Lighthouse, near Apalachicola, Florida, came to naught in the fall of 2005, when the battered tower collapsed into the Gulf of Mexico. That same year, Hurricane Katrina blasted lighthouses all along the Gulf of Mexico, especially in Louisiana, where the most notable lighthouses vanished – the reason why no Louisiana lighthouses are included here.

The American Lighthouse Foundation, the U.S. Lighthouse Association, and other such groups across America, are attempting to save the nation's remaining historic lighthouses. Their work is important, not only because lighthouses are part of America's history, but also because they are important to the safety of mariners at sea. By reading this book, and seeing for yourself just how interesting and beautiful these lighthouses can be, you may even be tempted to lend a hand yourself.

ALABAMA

*A*lthough it has little more than 50 miles of coast, Alabama, located in America's deep south, has a rich maritime tradition. Protected by a line of barrier islands, Alabama's Mobile Bay has long offered an attractive and safe anchorage for vessels seeking refuge from the storms of the Gulf of Mexico. Spanish ships first visited the bay during the early 1500s, and were followed, over the centuries, by the ships of many other nations.

In 1702 the French built a fort on a strategic site at the northern end of the bay, and the settlement that sprang up around it soon became the thriving port of Mobile. Freighters arriving at the city's wharves, to be loaded with cotton and other southern agricultural products, found that reaching the city was no easy task. Squeezed between low, sandy islands, the narrow entrance to Mobile Bay was as difficult to find as it was dangerous to navigate, while beyond the entrance, ships were forced to negotiate shoals and shallows. These were all but impossible to chart, since they shifted position with each passing storm.

Obviously, Alabama was in desperate need of lights to guide ships along the coast, into the bay, and into the safe harbor at Mobile. Unfortunately, many fine vessels would be lost and their crews marooned or drowned before Alabama's first lighthouse was constructed in 1821. The lighthouse, which proved of little use to navigators, was a modest 40-ft stone structure, built beside the walls of Fort Morgan, guarding Mobile Bay. Eventually it was replaced by taller and more effective light towers, both on Mobile Point and on Sand Island on the opposite side of the harbor entrance, while to the north, lesser but nonetheless vital maritime lights were added to point the way to the docks at Mobile.

Three of Alabama's historic lighthouses – Sand Island, Mobile Point, and the Mobile Island Lights – remain standing; these are all too vulnerable from the ravages of time and weather, but Alabamans, proud of their maritime heritage, are fighting to save these venerable structures.

MOBILE POINT LIGHT
Gulf Shores, Alabama

Shot to pieces by Admiral Farragut's gunboats during the Civil War

Somewhat belatedly, the U.S. government, recognizing the danger to shipping entering Mobile Bay, established a maritime light at Fort Morgan in 1821. It was built by private contractors, at a cost of only $8,995, but from the point of view of sea captains, waiting to be guided by its relatively weak beam, it was worth even less. Little more than four-stories-tall, the tower barely peeked over the walls of the fort, and its beacon could be seen from a distance of only about ten miles. Since Alabama's substantial coastal shoals extended at least that far into the Gulf of Mexico, more than a few mariners ran their vessels aground without ever having seen the light.

Hoping to correct this problem and improve the beacon, maritime officials hired contractor Winslow Lewis, an old seaman himself, to intensify the light. Lewis installed a lamp-and-reflector optic of his own design, and although he claimed a visibility of 30 miles, it made scant difference to the effectiveness of the beacon. Following construction of

the soaring light tower, built on nearby Sand Island in 1838, the Mobile Point Lighthouse was downgraded to a harbor light, used for guiding military vessels to Fort Morgan.

At the beginning of the Civil War, Confederate forces took charge of Fort Morgan and its lighthouse, holding them until Admiral David Farragut's attack on Mobile Bay in 1864. As Farragut's warships charged through the entrance and into the bay, their mighty guns trained on Fort Morgan, the hapless lighthouse was reduced to a pile of shattered masonry and bricks. The fallen tower was not replaced until 1873, well after the end of the war, when a 30-ft black steel tower, equipped with a fourth-order Fresnel lens, was erected. It remained in use until 1966.

SAND ISLAND LIGHT
Gulf Shores, Alabama

Lonely survivor of countless hurricanes

In 1838, the U.S. Lighthouse Service established a major station on Sand Island, to support an already existing maritime light at Mobile Point, on the opposite side of the entrance to Mobile Bay. Built atop a ring of piles by contractor Winslow Lewis, the Sand

Island tower was 55ft tall, and was equipped with one of Lewis's lamp-and-reflector optics. But the station's beacon proved only moderately effective at guiding vessels into the bay and, more importantly, warning them of Alabama's dangerous coastal shoals.

By the 1850s, American shipping interests had grown weary of sacrificing lives and profits to shipwrecks, and were demanding better service from the nation's outmoded system of coastal lights. To provide this, the government called on young, technically sophisticated military men, such as Daniel Leadbetter, a U.S. Army engineer. The station needed a much taller tower, which would enable the Sand Island beacon to to be seen by vessels before they struck the shoals. Completed in 1858, Leadbetter's Sand Island tower soared to a height of almost 200ft, making it one of the tallest brick lighthouses ever built.

The giant tower served for only a few years, however, for in 1861, during the opening months of the Civil War, Confederate authorities extinguished the light, removing the station's massive Fresnel lens. Soon the lighthouse fell into Union hands, and to prevent their enemies from using it as a watchtower, a small Confederate raiding party landed on Sand Island, where they stacked barrels of gunpowder in the tower and blew it up. Ironically, the official report on the successful raid was addressed to none other than Daniel Leadbetter, who by that time was a Confederate general.

Sand Island became the site of another, only slightly less impressive lighthouse in 1873, when the existing 131-ft brick tower was completed. Thanks in part to its powerful first-order Fresnel lens, the beacon was able to reach ships as far as 20 miles from the shore. Mariners were invariably relieved to see the light, but especially so in fast-deteriorating conditions.

This stretch of the Gulf of Mexico coast is periodically blasted by gales, and the Sand Island lighthouse has survived many hurricanes. In 1906, one such titanic storm carried away the keeper's house, along with the keeper and his wife – even washing away Sand Island itself. Although the island on which it was built had now vanished, the sturdy tower remained standing, just as it does today, a lonely sentinel rising from the waves of the Gulf.

The original Sand Island Light was completed in 1858, its short life ending during the Civil War when Confederates blew it up to keep it from falling into Union hands. The present, less impressive lighthouse was built in 1873.

BELOW & OPPOSITE: This charming lighthouse, resembling a small cottage, marks a safe channel through the muddy waters of Mobile Bay.

MOBILE MIDDLE BAY LIGHT
Mobile, Alabama

A cottage on stilts

As the economy of Alabama and the south recovered from the ravages of the Civil War, shipping passing through Mobile Bay began to increase, so much

so that, by the 1880s, it had become necessary to mark the safest channel by means of a permanent lighthouse. Since the tower had to be built in open water, it was placed on piles, set deep into the muddy bottom of the bay. In this case, 'tower' may be something of an exaggeration, since it was little more than a cottage, with a lantern room perched on its roof.

Poised a dozen feet or more above the choppy waters of the bay, the isolated, octagonal building has been home to several keepers over the years, one of them having lived here with his wife and two small children. It is said that since the infants needed milk, a cow was brought in and hoisted onto the elevated catwalk, where it munched hay and constantly mooed.

Its light deactivated during the 1960s, the Mobile Middle Bay Lighthouse might well have been demolished or left to rot, had it not been for the prodigious efforts of concerned Mobile and Alabama citizens who, with the help of private donations, government grants, and the hard work of volunteers, were able to save the station. Thankfully, to the relief of pleasure boaters and commercial shipping alike, the station's light has been recently restored.

CALIFORNIA

*C*alifornia's maritime history stretches back to the 18th century, when Spanish treasure ships regularly crossed the Pacific, from the Philippines, in search of Mexico's west-coast ports. More than a few veered off-course, bumping unexpectedly into California itself, usually with disastrous results. Spanish mariners dreaded the rugged California coast, that invariably lay hidden behind vast banks of fog, waiting to tear their fragile timber hulls apart.

In the early days of western exploration, California was thought to be an island, and in a very real sense it was, in that it had been cut off from the more settled regions of North America by an ocean of trackless desert. The only practical way to reach this remote but wondrous place was by sea. It should come as no surprise then, that the earliest settlers are thought to have established California's first maritime light. Each night they banked up an enormous fire, high up on the cliffs of Point Loma, so that Spanish freighters and military ships would be guided to the then tiny port of San Diego.

But the creation of a truly effective system of maritime lights would not come until after the United States took control of California during the 1840s. In 1849, a major federal survey of the western coast called for a chain of navigation lights, extending from the Puget Sound, Washington state, all the way southward to the Mexican border. To undertake the enormous task of building all these lighthouses, the government hired contractors from the east, including Francis Gibbons of Baltimore, who sailed around Cape Horn, reaching California with a shipload of supplies. By 1854, Gibbons had completed the west's first lighthouse on Alcatraz Island in San Francisco Bay, and more lighthouses appeared at Point Loma and Point Pinos, near Monterey, which exist to this day. Although he successfully fulfilled his contract, Gibbons lost money on the venture, largely because of a hidden wreck that claimed the Oriole, his supply ship.

Over the years, some 40 lighthouses were built along California's 800-mile coastline, more than half of which remain intact. Many of these historic towers – most of them dating from the 19th century – are accessible. With a few exceptions, they bear little resemblance to lighthouses either in the east or along the Great Lakes. Built according to strict budgets, California lighthouses are likely to be more compact structures, combining a keeper's dwelling with a relatively short tower. The dramatic topography of coastal California, where mountains drop directly into the sea, frequently made it unnecessary to construct lofty towers; here, many lighthouses gain all the elevation they need from their sites, perched high on soaring bluffs, overlooking the Pacific, or on the edges of precipitous cliffs. These spectacular settings are often as beautiful and interesting to the visitor as the lighthouses themselves.

OLD POINT LOMA LIGHT
San Diego, California

This lofty light could once be seen either 40 miles out at sea or not at all

Since height increases the range of maritime beacons, an elevated site is nearly always preferred: this was not the case at Point Loma. The combination tower and keeper's dwelling, built by Francis Gibbons during the mid-1850s, stands at an elevation of more than 400ft. Because of this, its beacon could often be seen from a considerable distance, sometimes from as much as 40 miles out in the Pacific Ocean. On the other hand, when fog rolled in, as it did and continues to do nearly every day along these shores, the light became trapped above the clouds and was rendered completely useless to sailors, situated low down on the surface of the sea.

Engineers never managed to solve this problem, as a result of which, the Old Point Loma Light enjoyed a relatively short active life of only about 35 years. By 1891, its light had been extinguished and it was replaced by a new lighthouse, built at a more practical elevation down at the base of the cliffs.

CALIFORNIA

*RIGHT & OPPOSITE: The New Point
Loma Light was built to replace the
older Point Loma Light that was
ineffective in fog.*

The original 160-year-old lighthouse still stands, however, and today serves as a popular attraction of the Cabrillo National Monument. Here visitors will find a simple stone Cape Cod-style cottage, built around a stout cylindrical tower – both exactly as they were when built by Francis Gibbons's skillful workmen. The highlight of any visit is a walk up the spiral staircase to the lantern room, which still houses a sparkling Fresnel lens.

(NEW) POINT LOMA LIGHT
San Diego, California

The favorite light of U.S. Navy sailors bound for San Diego

Built in 1891 to replace the often ineffective Old Point Loma Lighthouse, this steel-skeleton tower rises 70ft above the waves of the Pacific Ocean. A white steel cylinder, located between the tower's heavily braced steel legs, houses a staircase that gives access to the lantern room. For more than a century, a fine third-order Fresnel lens focused the station's beacon, but in 2002 it was removed and replaced by a more modern optic.

Oceanside

Rancho Santa Fe

Del Mar

La Jolla   SAN DIEGO

Pacific
Ocean   **CALIFORNIA**

Located on an active military base, the Point Loma Light is rarely accessible to visitors. However, it can be seen from a nearby parking area in the nearby Cabrillo National Monument, where the station's original lens is on display.

POINT PINOS LIGHT
Pacific Grove, California

The oldest light in California

California's oldest operating lighthouse marks the southern limit of Monterey Bay, a 40-mile-wide, semicircular indentation along the state's central coast. Like several other early Californian maritime sentinels, this was also built by Francis Gibbons during the 1850s. As with most of his other California lighthouses, Gibbons designed the Point Pinos Lighthouse to be a compact structure, its 43-ft tower rising straight through the roof of the station's Cape Cod-style keeper's dwelling.

The station was completed and commissioned for service in 1855, and its simple though comfortable residence has been home to a number of fascinating people over the years. One of these was Emily Fish, a former San Francisco socialite, who lived and

worked here for nearly two decades, having fallen on hard times. With the help of a loyal Chinese servant, Fish maintained the light and frequently

played host to local notables.

Monterey Bay and the old Spanish town of Monterey are particularly rich in marine life and maritime history.

They have long attracted fishing boats, ships, and adventurers to the area. One of the latter was the noted British author, Robert Louis Stevenson, who

OPPOSITE & ABOVE: Built in the 1850s, Point Pinos is the oldest lighthouse still operating in America.

visited the lighthouse and is said to have begun his famous novel, *Treasure Island*, while in Monterey. Interestingly, Stevenson was related to a number of Scottish lighthouse engineers.

Remarkably, the Point Pinos Light continues to operate more than 150 years after it first began to guide mariners. Flashing seaward every few seconds, the beacon guards Seal Point, a rugged jumble of rocks, washed over by the sea, that threatens vessels rounding the Monterey Peninsula and the entrance to the bay.

EAST BROTHER ISLAND LIGHT
Richmond, California

A working lighthouse and an attractive B & B

Established in 1874, it was intended that the East Brother Island Light should guide vessels through the narrow and often dangerous channel linking San Francisco Bay with the Sacramento river estuary. The most suitable location for the lighthouse proved to be a tiny island at the entrance to the San Pablo Straits, a few miles north-east of San Francisco.

The island was so small, however, that there was barely room for a light

tower and fog-signal building, let alone a residence for the keeper. Nonetheless, they managed to squeeze one of the most beautiful lighthouses in the western United States onto the half-acre property. To save space, the builders gave

the island a combination tower and dwelling. The blueprints that were produced were in fact very similar to those prepared for the Point Fermin Lighthouse, also completed in 1874. Consequently, both the Point Fermin

OPPOSITE & ABOVE: The beautiful East Brother Light is situated on an island site at the entrance to the San Pablo Straits.

and East Brother Island lighthouses are richly Victorian in style, with plenty of elaborate gingerbread trim.

The Coast Guard automated the light in 1967, and soon afterwards decided to tear down the historic tower and residence; but thanks to protests from local history buffs, the structure was saved. To raise money for its maintenance, the old building has been turned into a unique bed-and-breakfast establishment. Here guests can enjoy

OPPOSITE & FAR LEFT: As well as being a functioning lighthouse, East Brother also offers bed-and-breakfast accommodation to visitors.

ABOVE: East Brother's fifth-order Fresnel lens.

LEFT: A decorative owl keeps watch outside the lighthouse.

good food and breathtaking views of San Francisco. They can also sample life in a working lighthouse by day, and at night stay within the lighthouse itself or in the original fog-signal building. The station's fifth-order light and fog signal remain in operation.

BATTERY POINT LIGHT
Crescent City, California

A survivor of the great tsunami of 1962

The California Gold Rush spurred a massive construction boom in the west in 1849, the material needed to sustain it being available on the densely-wooded slopes of coastal mountains in northern California, where redwood grew in wondrous abundance. To take advantage of this 'red gold,' freighters began to crowd into the bustling harbors of small lumber towns, such as Crescent City, located only a few miles south of the Oregon border. To guide them safely to port, the government ordered the construction of a lighthouse in the vicinity during the 1850s.

Like several other California lighthouses, built at this time, Battery Point Light was the work of Francis Gibbons, who completed it in 1856. Poised on stony Battery Point, near the

entrance to the harbor, it closely resembles other Gibbons lighthouses, and features a rectangular granite residence with a relatively short brick tower pushing through its roof. The tower is only 37ft tall, but its lofty position enables its light to shine forth from an elevation of nearly 300ft.

When an earthquake in Alaska sent a mighty tsunami hurtling toward California in 1962, the station's keepers must have been thankful that their home was so far above water. The tidal wave struck Battery Point with unimaginable force, but its waters were not quite high enough to reach the lighthouse.

After more than a century of service to mariners, the Battery Point beacon was extinguished in 1965. However, it was relit and returned to service as a private aid to navigation in 1982. Nowadays, the facility is maintained by the local historical society.

POINT BONITA LIGHT
San Francisco, California

Linked to the mainland by a miniature Golden Gate Bridge

Completed in 1855, the original Point Bonita Lighthouse once stood on a cliff more than 300ft above the sea. Its

considerable elevation gave the beacon tremendous range, but as with the lofty Old Point Loma Light, near San Diego, it was frequently rendered ineffective by fog. In time, maritime officials decided to establish another light at a more practical elevation. Completed in 1872, the replacement tower, and its adjacent fog-signal house, were

obviously the work of brave and fearless men, since the construction site was located on a knife-edge of rock, that dropped more than 100ft down into the pounding surf.

As if to emphasize the precariousness of the site, the path linking the lighthouse to the mainland collapsed into the sea during the 1940s,

OPPOSITE: Battery Point was built to guide shipping into the small lumber town of Crescent City.

ABOVE: Point Bonita sits precariously on a rocky outcrop. It was built in 1872, replacing an earlier light that proved ineffective in fog.

making it necessary for the Coast Guard to build a handsome wooden suspension bridge – a kind of miniature of the nearby Golden Gate Bridge – to provide access to the tower and fog-signal equipment.

Since it points the way to the Golden Gate, and onward to the major ports of San Francisco and Oakland, the Point Bonita Light is rightly considered to be one of the most important maritime beacons in the west. Signalling out toward the Pacific from an elevation of 124ft, it powerful light is still focused by the second-order Fresnel lens, installed here in 1877. The light can be seen from distances of up to 18 miles out at sea.

POINT REYES LIGHT
Point Reyes National Seashore, California

The foggiest place in America

To the north of San Francisco, the headlands of Point Reyes extend out 10 miles into the Pacific Ocean, presenting one of the most dangerous obstacles to navigation along America's entire western coast. The threat to mariners is made all the more acute by the fact that the jagged rocks are shrouded in fog for

much of the time. Although more than a few vessels were lost here during and after the Gold Rush years, the point had no navigational beacon to warn mariners until 1871. Construction of the Point Reyes Lighthouse was long-delayed, largely because of the difficulty of erecting buildings on the local cliffs.

Covered in a dreary blanket of fog for an average of 110 days a year, and

OPPOSITE, ABOVE LEFT & ABOVE: The headland at Point Reyes extends 10 miles out into the Pacific Ocean, presenting a dangerous obstacle that is made even more treacherous by the dense fog that frequently enshrouds the area.

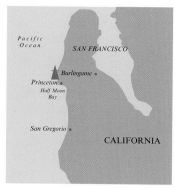

arriving at Point Reyes National Seashore.

POINT MONTARA LIGHT
Pacifica, California

The old keeper's residence now serves as a youth hostel

ABOVE: Some of the inner workings of Point Reyes Light, including foghorns and generator.

FAR RIGHT: Point Montara Light guides shipping negotiating this hazardous coastline, where many tragic shipwrecks have occurred.

often exposed to high winds, Point Reyes was never a popular posting as far as keepers were concerned; it is said that some became so depressed by the conditions that they were driven to contemplate suicide. In spite of this, full-time keepers continued to maintain the station for more than a century – in fact, right up until the light was deactivated in 1975.

The Point Reyes beacon was focused by an enormous first-order Fresnel lens during its active years; the massive lens had 16 bull's-eyes, or convex focal points, throwing powerful beams of light out over the ocean like spokes in a giant wheel. The light appeared to flash as the lens rotated, the beams coming into the line of sight of sailors at sea. Today, the big lens remains in the Point Reyes tower, where it serves as an historic relic of considerable interest to visitors

Located on the San Francisco peninsula, and guarding the southern approach to San Francisco Bay, about 25 miles south of San Francisco itself, Point Montara was the site of several tragic shipwrecks during the 1860s and early 1870s, caused by the prevalence of fog in the area. One of the losses was that of the freighter, *Acuelo*, which came to grief on rocks not far from the point in 1872. The freighter and its cargo of coal and iron were valued in excess of $150,000 – far more than building and maintaining a light station on the point would have cost. Thus, as far as western maritime interests were concerned, it seemed both reasonable and economical to establish a fog signal here in 1872, even though no lighthouse was built at Point Montara until 1900.

The original lighthouse, built to work in association with the fog signal, consisted of a simple wooden tower, and

an equally modest keeper's dwelling, built on the edge of the Point Montara cliffs; in 1928, the original tower was replaced by the 30-ft cast-iron structure that marks the point today, its light visible for a distance of 14 miles out at sea. Nowadays, the century-old Victorian-style keeper's residence also serves as a youth hostel.

POINT VICENTE LIGHT
Los Angeles, California

Beloved of Hollywood moviemakers

More than a few scenes from movies and television commercials have been shot against the backdrop of the handsome Point Vicente Lighthouse, which is understandable, given its glamorous location among swaying palms on the Palos Verdes peninsula. Here, the attractive cross-hatched windows of the lantern room, that surmounts the gleaming white tower, seem to emit a golden glow when touched by the rays of the setting sun.

The Point Vicente tower, built during the 1920s, was never intended for such frivolity, however, but for the serious task of guiding ships, preventing wrecks, and saving lives – all of which it has

LIGHTHOUSES OF AMERICA

OPPOSITE, LEFT & PAGES 36–37. The Point Vicente Light's romantic looks have made it a favorite setting for movies and commercials. More important, however, is the fact that it has been saving lives for over 80 years.

performed most effectively for more than 80 years.

The 67-ft reinforced-concrete tower provides only about a third of the beacon's 185-ft elevation; the rest is provided by the cliff on which the lighthouse stands. It is thanks to this natural advantage, and to the power of the station's still-active third-order Fresnel lens, rated at 437,000 candlepower, that the Point Vicente beacon can be seen from a distance of more than 20 miles. Interestingly, the classic crystal lens, in use here since 1926, previously saw service in a lighthouse in Alaska for almost 40 years.

PIGEON POINT LIGHT
Pescadera, California

A brick titan, located to the south of San Francisco

Most California light towers are short, compared with their counterparts in the east, which was not the case as far as this giant is concerned. Located some 50 miles south of San Francisco, the Pigeon Point Light marks a particularly dangerous stretch of coast, where more than a few ships have come to grief. Among these was the clipper, *Carrier Pigeon*, which ended its days on the

rocks not far from the headland in 1853. Originally known as Punta de las Balenas (Whale Point), because the area is often frequented by gray whales during their migration periods, it was renamed Pigeon Point to commemorate the tragic wreck.

BELOW: Because no elevated site was available in the area, Pigeon Point's tower was made uncharacteristically tall for a west-coast light.

CALIFORNIA

BELOW: Pigeon Point Light.

FAR RIGHT: Point Arena Light. The original tower was irreparably damaged by the San Francisco earthquake, making it necessary for it to be demolished in 1906 and replaced with another made of reinforced concrete.

To prevent further losses of this kind, the government established a light station here in 1872, but because the area offered no suitable high-elevation construction sites, the station was given a 115-ft tower of its own. The builders used brick brought from the east, which meant that a ship was obliged to sail almost 12,000 miles around Cape Horn to reach the site.

To provide the necessary power, the station was assigned an enormous first-order crystal Fresnel lens. This has served the station for more than a century, and though it is still in place, it is no longer active. Since 1972, Pigeon Point has been using a modern aerobeacon, positioned on the outside of the lantern room.

POINT ARENA LIGHT
Point Arena, California

Built to withstand even the mightiest of earthquakes

The same great earthquake that destroyed San Francisco in 1906 also devastated the lighthouse that had marked Point Arena since 1870. A look at the geology of the area makes it easy to understand why the structure was so vulnerable: the rocks that tumble into the sea, below the point, are tortured and scarred, indicating that the notorious San Andreas Fault, that has generated so many destructive California earthquakes, veers off into the Pacific Ocean where Point Arena is located.

When government inspectors visited the station after the 1906 tremor, they found that the walls of the light tower had been shattered, damaging the station's Fresnel lens. Within two years the crippled tower had been pulled down and replaced by a reinforced-concrete structure, built to withstand even greater earthquakes than the one that had destroyed the original. Shaped rather like a spindle, the tower rises above the point some 115ft into the sky. The height of the tower, together with the elevation of its site, places the station more than 150ft above the Pacific. Flashing white every 15 seconds, its light can be seen for a distance of up to 25 miles out at sea.

Point Arena's original first-order Fresnel lens, weighing more than a ton, no longer operates. It has been left in place for historical reasons, its task having been transferred to a modern optic, located on the outside of the lantern room.

POINT SUR LIGHT
Big Sur, California

The enormous dirigible, Macon, *once crashed into the sea nearby*

OPPOSITE: Point Arena Light and its internal spiral staircase.

BELOW: The Point Sur Light protects shipping from a beautiful but hazardous coastline.

CALIFORNIA

BELOW: *Point Sur Light.*

OPPOSITE: *Trinidad Head Light. This is a replica constructed for tourists to visit, the actual light being inaccessible to the public, located 200ft up a cliff.*

To the south of Monterey, a range of mile-high mountains drop precipitously into the Pacific Ocean. Popularly known as the Big Sur, this extraordinarily rugged, 70-mile-long stretch of central Californian coast offers some of the most spectacular scenery on the planet. It also threatens vessels, straying too close to shore, with almost certain destruction. For this reason, mariners usually avoid the area completely, keeping well out into the ocean to avoid the Sur's hull-crushing rocks.

To warn navigators of these dangers, the government established a major light station on Point Sur in 1889. Essentially an offshore mountain, linked to the mainland by a slender thread of beach, Point Sur presented builders with a daunting task, and before construction could begin, a special railroad had to be built to bring in supplies; then the granite blocks and other building materials, had to be lugged up to the 350-ft summit. Building the lighthouse took more than two years and cost the U.S. Treasury more than $100,000 – a substantial sum at the time.

The Point Sur Lighthouse turned out to be as difficult to maintain as it had been to build. The station's isolation made it lonely for the keepers and their families, and the work of tending the light was physically taxing: every night, keepers had to climb almost 400 steps to reach the lantern room and light the lamps. Theirs was a vital task, however, since the Point Sur Light undoubtedly saved countless vessels. One the light could not save, however, was the U.S.S. *Macon*, a mighty naval dirigible that was sunk in a storm here in 1935.

TRINIDAD HEAD LIGHT
Trinidad, California

A memorial to mariners lost at sea

When travelers visit the quaint fishing village of Trinidad, and see the lighthouse there, what they are in fact looking at is a replica. The real lighthouse cannot be seen from the village, because it is located on the far side of a nearby mountain.

Trinidad Head Light was built in 1871, into the face of a precipitous cliff about 200ft above the Pacific Ocean. Its beacon was intended to serve both as a harbor light for Trinidad itself and as a coastal light to guide lumber freighters shuttling between the mills in northern California and markets in San Francisco and beyond.

Although it was equipped with a relatively small fourth-order Fresnel lens, the station's considerable elevation gave the beacon a hefty boost, and it could often be seen for 20 miles out at sea. When the station was automated in 1974, the lens was removed and located in the replica of the original tower in Trinidad village. This also houses the station's old fog bell, as well as a plaque inscribed with the names of local mariners who lost their lives at sea.

CONNECTICUT

*T*he *first Dutch and English settlements took root along the New England coast during the early 1600s, since when it has been a haunt of mariners, their ships sailing in and out of the snug harbors along America's north-eastern coast.*

The ports that line Connecticut's shores, however, do not look out unhindered toward the east and the Atlantic Ocean, but southward onto the waters of Long Island Sound. Although relatively calm and shallow, the sound is nonetheless a substantial body of water, and can be fraught with many dangers. More than 100 miles long and dozens of miles wide, it is frequently assaulted by storms or enshrouded in fog. There are many shoals here, and long stretches of the shore are difficult, if not impossible, to distinguish from open water; consequently the sound has claimed thousands of vessels and countless lives throughout the centuries.

The difficulty in navigating Long Island Sound may be the reason why Connecticut was among the first of the original colonies to establish a major coastal beacon. Completed in 1760, the maritime tower, built at New London, was only the fourth lighthouse to be built in what would later become the United States, while earlier lighthouses were constructed at Boston, Brant Point on Nantucket, and Beavertail on Rhode Island.

In time, a sparkling chain of lights would mark the Connecticut shore from Stonington in the east to Stamford, where the sound begins to narrow sharply. Most of these lights have since been extinguished, but many of the historic towers still stand as reminders of Connecticut's vibrant maritime past. Fortunately for those who love lighthouses, and appreciate maritime history, the New London Lighthouse can be counted among Connecticut's foremost survivors.

NEW LONDON HARBOR LIGHT

New London, Connecticut

This colonial veteran still shines forth after 250 years

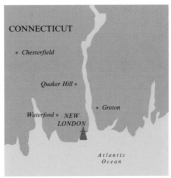

FAR LEFT & PAGE 46: *The original tower of the New London Harbor Light was erected in 1760. The one seen today, however, was built in 1801 and has occupied a bank of the River Thames ever since.*

PAGE 47: *In spite of being surrounded by water, the New London Ledge Light has the appearance of a small, three-story mansion, similar to those that once lined the Connecticut shore.*

Rising proudly from the banks of the Thames river, the white, octagonal tower of the New London Harbor Light looks much the same today as it did when it was built more than two centuries ago. This is no dusty monument to America's colonial past, however, and having served mariners for nearly a quarter of a millennium, it remains a living, fully-functioning lighthouse to this day.

In 1760, the station was established with funds raised by means of a colonial lottery. The existing tower replaced the original structure in 1801, and it has changed little since that time. The station still utilizes its fourth-order Fresnel lens, that was placed in situ in 1857, the white beacon flashing on and off in six-second intervals. Navigators approaching the harbor entrance are warned away from the dangerous shoals by a red light.

The New London Light was among the first major coastal beacons in the United States to be automated. Timers were installed in the tower in 1912,

making the need for a full-time keeper unnecessary; the keeper's former dwelling was sold as a private residence that same year.

NEW LONDON LEDGE LIGHT
New London, Connecticut

A haunted offshore mansion

The New London Ledge Lighthouse, with its elaborate French Empire styling, is certainly remarkable if not unique. Built in 1910 in open water, and directly above a threatening shoal, this unusual structure was intended not only to warn mariners, but also to exude an elegance similar to that of the aristocratic mansions, that once lined the Connecticut shore. Many of these beautiful homes were destroyed when a great hurricane ripped into this part of New England in 1938. Fortunately, the lighthouse survived.

Seeing it from a distance gives the rather haunting impression of a building that has somehow broken away from the shore and floated out into the harbor. Perhaps not surprisingly, the lighthouse is reputed to be haunted by the ghost of a former keeper, who committed suicide when his wife left him for another man.

Automated in 1987, the station now guides mariners by means of its solar-powered modern beacon and automatic fog signal.

DELAWARE

DELAWARE

*D*elaware can claim a long and significant maritime history. Explored by Henry Hudson in 1609, it was the site of successive colonizations by Swedish, Dutch, and English immigrants, who settled the area during the 1680s. One of these was the English Quaker, William Penn, who went on to found Pennsylvania in 1682. Delaware broke away from Pennsylvania in 1704, due partly to the rivalry that existed between its bustling ports of Wilmington and Philadelphia, located further up the Delaware river. From the very start, Delaware was dependent on trade, and the calm waters of the broad Delaware Bay attracted a steady stream of freighters headed for the wharves at Wilmington, or seeking refuge from fierce Atlantic storms. Beacons like the Brandywine Shoal Light, at Lewes, have continued to point the way since the mid-19th century.

Although only 28 miles of the Delaware coastline actually borders the Atlantic Ocean, it once had a dozen or more active lighthouses. Several of these remain in service, and unlike many still in operation elsewhere, they continue to be of benefit to commercial shipping, marking the safe channel through Delaware Bay, one of the nation's busiest maritime highways.

Delaware has one major light facing onto the sea, emanating from Fenwick Island on the Maryland border. Most people are unaware that the famous Mason-Dixon Line, that supposedly separated the northern states from the south, originated as a survey made of the Maryland-Delaware border. The line runs straight through the land on which Fenwick Island Lighthouse stands.

FENWICK ISLAND LIGHT
Fenwick Island, Delaware

Marking the border between north and south

The federal Lighthouse Board was very active during the 1850s, establishing many new lights to fill dark, previously unmarked stretches of coast. One of

these new lighthouses was built on Fenwick Island, on the Maryland-Delaware border.

Comprising an 84-ft masonry tower and a two-story wood-frame keeper's residence, the Fenwick Island Light has changed very little since it was completed in 1858. Like several other lighthouses on the east coast, it has double walls, a design feature that is most likely the reason for the tower's long service life. The tower remains sound and its beacon continues to shine after 150 years of battering by storms. The station's original third-order Fresnel lens remains in service to this day.

BRANDYWINE SHOAL LIGHT
Lewes, Delaware

An historic beacon that is now powered by the sun

Over the last two centuries, several different lighthouses or lightships have guarded the dangerous Brandywine Shoal in Delaware Bay. One of these was an extraordinary structure – quite unlike anything built before or since. The Brandywine Shoal Light, that was actually in New Jersey waters, was an experimental lighthouse built in 1850. It

it was replaced by a caisson-style lighthouse. Having resisted both ice and the tides for nearly a century, the 60-ft caisson tower still remains in use. The station's automated beacon is now powered by batteries recharged daily by means of solar panels.

OPPOSITE BELOW CENTER & LEFT: The Fenwick Island Light was built in 1858 and remains sound and functional to this day.

BELOW: The Brandywine Shoal Light is now solar-powered.

consisted of a rather short, cone-shaped tower, resting on a forest of blade-like piles that had literally been screwed into the mud beneath the bay. There were so many piles that they formed a sort of protective fence, that were able to shield the lighthouse from the massive ice floes that often filled the bay in winter.

The experiment proved successful, and the structure lasted until 1914, when

FLORIDA

*W*hen Juan Ponce de Leon, the Spanish adventurer, landed on the south-eastern coast of North America in April 1513, he was searching for the fabled Fountain of Youth. Instead he found a peninsula, which he named Pascua de Florida or 'Feast of Flowers.' This beautiful name suggests he was oblivious of the dangers that lay in wait for explorers and mariners alike. Ponce de Leon himself would later die from an arrow wound, dealt him by a native Floridian warrior, but thousands upon thousands of mariners and explorers would lose their lives in other ways.

But the arrows of outraged Native Americans were never Florida's primary threat – rather the arrow-shaped peninsula itself. Extending more than 400 miles from the south-eastern corner of the North American continent, it thrusts itself into one of the busiest and most important shipping routes in the world. Entire fleets have vanished along Florida's low, almost invisible coastline, also in the Florida Keys – the chain of sandy coral islands that drop like a fishhook into the hurricane-prone straits below the peninsula.

When the United States acquired Florida from the Spanish in 1819, federal maritime officials got to know these hazards only too well. More than a few U.S. Navy fighting ships and merchant vessels were lost to Florida's shoals and coral reefs, and to make the waters off Florida's deadly coasts safer for navigation, the government began to build lighthouses almost at once. Among the first were the impressive towers at St. Augustine and Pensacola and the lesser lights at Key West, Sand Key and Garden Key – all built during the 1820s; many more Florida light stations would be established in the 1830s and during the mid-19th century after the Lighthouse Board took charge of the U.S. system of maritime lights.

Florida's sweltering climate and marshy terrain confronted designers and construction crews with challenges never faced elsewhere. In some areas, such as on the sea-swept reefs of the Keys, lighthouse construction was thought to be all but impossible. But as is often the case, when necessity has to overcome insurmountable obstacles, human ingenuity and determination rise to the challenge. During the 1850s, the government turned to innovative young military engineers, such as George Meade, to complete the dark gaps in the chain of maritime beacons guarding the nation's coasts and shipping lanes.

In the Keys, Meade developed a whole new way of building lighthouses, erecting giant steel skeleton towers and anchoring them to corrosion-resistant corrugated piles, driven deep into the sand and coral. The skeleton towers had open walls, that allowed hurricane-force winds to pass through them without harming the structure. One of the many great ironies of the Civil War was that this lighthouse builder, who had done so much to assist what was decidedly a southern state, would later command the north's Army of the Potomac. It was General George Meade who engineered the Union battle plan at Gettysburg, turning the tide of the war decisively against the Confederacy.

ST. AUGUSTINE LIGHT
St. Augustine, Florida

This, the oldest Floridian maritime beacon, marks the former Spanish capital

When federal officials paid their first visit to St. Augustine, shortly after the U.S. took control of Florida in 1819, they found in the former Spanish capital an old stone tower. Some said it was only a watchtower, while others claimed

OPPOSITE BELOW RIGHT, LEFT & BELOW: St. Augustine's present light was completed in 1874, having replaced two previous structures.

that a light shining from its uppermost level had once been used as a harbor marker. Whatever its original purpose had been, the tower was soon pressed into service as a makeshift lighthouse. A lantern hung from its walls provided vessels bound for St. Augustine with all the guidance they would receive, until a more conventional lighthouse was completed in 1823. A 73-ft tower, fitted with oil lamps and reflectors, this new sentinel proved little more effective than the one it replaced. The beacon was so weak that it could reach ships only a short distance beyond the harbor limits.

Despite its inadequacy, the new tower remained in use for half a century. Unlike many other southern lighthouses, it also survived the Civil War, but in the end would prove no match against tidal erosion. By the 1870s, the structure was a hopeless wreck, and the Lighthouse Board ordered construction of a replacement. Completed in 1874, the

new 165-ft tower was a fine structure, considered quite modern for its time. Fitted with a massive first-order Fresnel lens, its lofty lantern room displayed a flashing beacon that could be seen from up to two dozen miles out at sea. Today,

after more than 130 years of service, the same spiral-striped tower and prismatic lens is still in use.

Unfortunately, it is difficult to protect lighthouses or any other historic property from vandals. In 1988, a

teenager, armed with a high-powered rifle, fired shots at the St. Augustine lantern room, seriously damaging its fine crystal lens. Private funds were raised to restore the lens, which took several years and more than $500,000 to repair.

OPPOSITE LEFT: The building was considered modern for its time.

OPPOSITE RIGHT & BELOW: St. Augustine is fitted with a huge Fresnel lens, recently restored after damage.

The first-order Fresnel lens, installed in the Pensacola Light in 1859, is still functional. It is visible for 25 miles or so out in the Gulf of Mexico.

PENSACOLA LIGHT
Pensacola, Florida

Guiding naval fighting ships for nearly two centuries

Far to the west of St. Augustine, near the tip of the Florida Panhandle, masons completed work on Florida's second lighthouse in 1824. This new beacon was of particular importance to U.S. interests in the Gulf of Mexico and the Caribbean, in that it served the key naval base at Pensacola. From here U.S. Navy fighting ships were able to block incursions by European powers into the Gulf region, while taking on marauding pirates in the Florida Keys.

The lighthouse that guided these warships in and out of harbor was a modest affair, being a 40-ft brick structure built by Winslow Lewis; it housed the same sort of inefficient lamp-and-reflector optic that found their way into most of Lewis's lighthouses. One thing that could be said for Lewis, however, was that the bills he submitted for his work were never exorbitant. Lewis charged the government only $5,275 for the Pensacola tower and lens, which, incidentally, he designed himself. Some may say that the facility was worth exactly what the U.S. Treasury

paid for it – and no more. Despite the relative weakness of its beacon, the Lewis lighthouse remained in use until shortly before the Civil War.

In 1859, on orders from the Lighthouse Board in Washington, a much more impressive tower was built at Pensacola. At 171ft, it remains to this day among the tallest brick towers ever constructed. The first-order Fresnel lens, that was installed in the tower at the time, is still in use, focusing an especially bright beacon that can be seen from the decks of ships 25 miles or so out in the Gulf of Mexico.

CAPE FLORIDA LIGHT
Key Biscayne, Florida

Attacked by Seminoles

To mark the south-eastern end of the Florida peninsula, the Cape Florida Light was established on Key Biscayne in 1835. It was in operation for less than a year, when war erupted with the Florida Seminoles, outraged at the loss of their lands to white settlers. In the spring of 1836, the exposed and isolated station was attacked by a large war party of Seminoles, who arrived in canoes and quickly overran the station. The keeper, John Thomson, was able to

survive the attack, by taking refuge in the lighthouse's stout brick tower, but the Seminoles burned the tower steps, leaving the scorched keeper stranded in the lantern room more than 60ft above ground. A U.S. Navy warship drove off the raiders, and Thomson was eventually rescued by sailors, who fired a line into the lantern room and lowered him to safety in a basket.

Repaired and raised in height to more than 90ft, the brick tower continued to serve mariners for more than 40 years. In 1878, however, a more useful offshore light was established at nearby Fowey Rocks, when the lamps at Cape Florida were extinguished. Afterwards, the Cape Florida tower was left unattended for more than a century, its badly weathered fabric left to slowly

ABOVE & PAGES 56–57: The Cape Florida Light marks the south-eastern end of the Florida peninsula. Left to decay for over 100 years, it was returned to use in the 1990s.

PAGE 57 RIGHT: Originally on Little Cumberland Island, Georgia, the lighthouse was dismantled and moved to Amelia Island in the 1830s.

crumble. During the 1990s, however, Florida preservationists made an all-out effort to save the old tower as a reminder of the state's early history, and more than $1.5 million in private and government funds were poured into its refurbishment. Not only were its walls shored up and repainted, but an active light was also placed in the lantern room, so that the historic lighthouse could once again fulfill the role for which it was intended.

AMELIA ISLAND LIGHT
Old Fernandina Beach, Florida

A Georgia lighthouse moved to Florida

During the 1830s, the government sought to brighten the long, dark stretches of coast, that caused seamen to be wary of Florida's eastern shores. With lights already shining at St. Augustine and Cape Florida, placing a beacon at the northern end of the peninsula, near the Georgia border, was thought to be a next logical step.

A site was selected on Amelia Island, near to the mouth of the St. Marys river, and a light station was established there in 1838. Instead of building a new tower, however, maritime officials had the lighthouse on Georgia's Little Cumberland Island dismantled and

FLORIDA

shipped to Amelia Island, where it was reassembled.

In 1885, the tower and the adjacent keeper's dwelling, that were now being used as a residence by Coast Guard personnel, were renovated in the Victorian style. Today, the station looks much the same as it did when the renovations were completed more than a century ago. The 64-ft brick tower is painted white, topped by a black metal lantern, and the station's flashing white beacon is still being focused by the same third-order Fresnel lens that was originally installed in 1857. The light also has a red sector, that is used to warn vessels approaching a bank of dangerous shoals lying in the nearby Nassau Sound.

PONCE DE LEON INLET LIGHT
Ponce de Leon Inlet, Florida

The old Mosquito Inlet light station is now a treasure trove of maritime artifacts

Like the original St. John's Lighthouse, the first light to be erected at Mosquito Inlet (known today as Ponce de Leon Inlet), did not survive for long. In fact, it had just been completed, when an attack by Seminole warriors in 1835 destroyed much of the station. Before it could be repaired, a hurricane knocked down the tower, which would not be replaced for more than half a century.

In 1885, government contractors arrived at the inlet and erected a massive tower on its banks. Built from red

LIGHTHOUSES OF AMERICA

bricks, shipped in from Maryland, the 168-ft tower was completed and began service in 1887. Fitted with a first-order Fresnel lens, imported from France, its light could be seen for more than 20 miles out in the Atlantic Ocean.

The station is still in operation, but nowadays serves another function as well. The grand old brick tower is now the focus of one of the finest maritime museums in America. Handsomely restored, the tower, the keeper's residences, and other station buildings,

FLORIDA

The spiral staircase at the Ponce de Leon Inlet Light.

have all been opened up to the public as part of the Ponce de Leon Inlet Lighthouse Museum. Among the highlights of its many attractions is an unrivaled display of lighthouse lenses, including the first-order Fresnel lens that was once in service at the Cape Canaveral Light.

CAPE CANAVERAL LIGHT
Cape Canaveral, Florida

A rocket-shaped tower marks the cape on which the Space Center now stands

Long before it received worldwide attention as the home of the U.S. space program, Cape Canaveral was known and dreaded by seamen as one of North America's deadliest coastal obstacles. Its strange, fragmented shape, like an irregular slice cut from the mainland, extends out and down into the open Atlantic, menacing vessels moving north or south along the east coast of Florida. Many mariners paid with their lives for sailing too close to the cape's shoals and shallows, and to warn navigators, the government established a light station

here in 1848. Considered inadequate, the original, relatively short Cape Canaveral tower was replaced by a much taller structure, shortly after the Civil War.

A 145-ft brick giant, the cape's second lighthouse was sturdily built and would have been guiding ships to this day, had it not been undermined by erosion. A third tower, built at a much safer distance from the Atlantic, took its place in 1893. The station's classic first-order Fresnel lens was removed and placed in a museum in 1993, and the beacon now functions with a modern optic. It is said that, during the 1960s, American scientists used to climb the Cape Canaveral tower to watch their rockets being blasted into orbit.

JUPITER INLET LIGHT
Jupiter, Florida

Men who co-operated in the establishment of this light went on to become rivals during the Civil War

Painted bright red, the 125-ft cylindrical tower of the Jupiter Lighthouse is one of the most spectacular and historic structures in America. Completed shortly before the Civil War, the lighthouse was decommissioned by Confederate troops, who removed its

huge lens, hiding it in the sand. The light was not restored to service until 1866, a year after the war ended, when a former keeper rediscovered the lens. Undamaged by its years buried in the sand, the lens was restored to its rightful place at the top of the Jupiter tower. Still in use today, the lens concentrates light so effectively that the beacon can be seen from more than two dozen miles out at sea.

The lighthouse has survived not only the ravages of time and war, but also of natural phenomena. Gales and hurricanes periodically attack this stretch of Florida's coast, including the one in 1928 that knocked out the electric power. The keeper responded to this emergency by re-installing the station's original oil lamps and rotating the lens by hand to keep the light flashing.

It is one of the strange ironies of the Civil War that Robert E. Lee, having been responsible for surveying the Jupiter Lighthouse property, and George Meade, having designed the structure itself, should eventually be forced to confront each other across Gettysburg's bloody battlefield. As commander of the Union Army of the Potomac, General Meade defeated the Confederates and averted General Lee's invasion of the north.

LEFT: This was the third lighthouse to be built to guard the treacherous obstacle that is Cape Canaveral itself, and which today is also famous as the home of the U.S. Space Center.

PAGES 62–63: The impressive Jupiter Light, built before the Civil War, has survived the ravages of time, war, and natural phenomena to function as an effective beacon to this day.

KEY WEST LIGHT
Key West, Florida

Once the haunt of pirates and buccaneers

Florida's early lighthouses were not all located on the mainland. In 1825, only months after the St. Augustine Light was commissioned, a maritime beacon was established at Key West, which, at that time, was a bustling frontier town, recently plagued by pirates. Shortly after the United States acquired Florida from Spain, the U.S. Navy arrived in force to evict the buccaneers and put a stop to their predatory attacks on American merchant ships. Being an island naval base, Key West now needed a powerful maritime beacon to guide naval warships in and out of port.

The lighthouse that the government built was better constructed than many early-19th-century examples, even though it was to serve mariners for little more than 20 years. In 1846, a mighty hurricane swept down on Key West, destroying the tower and keeper's residence along with much of the town.

Within a year, a second lighthouse was completed on a less vulnerable site, and having been substantially renovated over the years, the structure still stands. The light was deactivated in 1969, but

has since been returned to service as a private aid to navigation. The tower and gracious keeper's bungalow are now open to the public as part of the Key West Lighthouse Museum.

SAND KEY LIGHT
Near Key West, Florida

Marking a hurricane black spot

Not long after the construction of the Key West Lighthouse in 1825, it was apparent that a second beacon was needed to warn mariners of the presence of nearby Sand Key. Rising only a few feet above the waves, Sand Key had no vegetation or structures of any kind visible on its surface, which made it a severe threat to shipping. The U.S. maritime authorities accordingly ordered the construction of a modest light tower and keeper's residence on this isolated key in 1827.

The station had been functioning adequately for almost 20 years, when a great hurricane swept out of the Caribbean in October 1846, devastating Key West and reducing its lighthouse to a state of ruin. At Sand Key, however, the storm left almost nothing behind. After the winds had subsided, a rescue party hastened to the key but could find no trace of the lighthouse, its keeper,

Sand Key by I.W.P. Lewis and built by army engineer, George Meade. It consisted of a 105-ft iron-skeleton tower, set atop a dozen stout pilings driven deep into the underlying sand and coral. The heavily-braced legs of the tower were strong enough to withstand the most powerful gales and hurricanes, and the tower remains as sound today as it was when it was built more than 150 years ago. A first-order Fresnel lens once focused the station's unusually bright beacon, but it was removed shortly before the Second World War. Nowadays, a modern optic produces a light that can be seen from a distance of about 20 miles.

ALLIGATOR REEF LIGHT
Matecumbe Key, Florida

Warns of a deadly ocean predator

Alligator Reef is a long way from the nearest alligator – a toothy reptile that prefers mainland lakes and rivers and is never seen in the salty waters off the Florida Keys. But the reef itself can also be described as a predator of sorts. In 1822, the U.S. Navy schooner, *Alligator*, came too close, was caught in the jaws of the reef, and sank. From then on, this treacherous, open-sea obstacle was known as Alligator Reef.

OPPOSITE LEFT: Key West Light now serves as part of the Key West Lighthouse Museum and as a private aid to navigation.

LEFT: The Alligator Reef Light was named for the U.S. Navy schooner, Alligator, *that was wrecked by the treacherous reef in 1822.*

Joseph Appleby, or his daughter and grandson, who happened to be on the island when the hurricane struck. In fact, Sand Key had all but vanished.

While much of the key had been swept into the ocean by the storm, a bank of deadly shoals and shallows remained to threaten ships; but to mark them with a maritime beacon required what would have been advanced engineering skills at that time. Such a lighthouse was nonetheless designed for

FLORIDA

Even after the tragic loss of the *Alligator*, which cost the lives of several men, no attempt was made to mark the reef until the 1870s, by which time several other ships had fallen victim to the reef. To prevent further losses, federal maritime authorities called upon its most innovative young engineers to design a structure for the difficult site. In response, they designed and built an iron-skeleton tower, anchoring it securely to subsurface piles. The keeper's living quarters were located in a building held safely above the waves by the tower's sturdy legs, while the station's lantern room, lamps and lens were situated at the very top of the tower, more than 130ft above the ocean.

The design was appropriate for a lighthouse located far from the shore, in a hurricane-prone latitude, but executing it proved costly. Construction of the tower cost the government $185,000 – a truly amazing sum at the time. But despite its hefty price tag, the lighthouse has turned out to be something of a bargain. It continues to warn ships more than 130 years after it was completed, its flashing white and red light visible from about 12 miles out at sea.

AMERICAN SHOAL LIGHT
Sugarloaf Key, Florida

A costly tower that has proven its worth

To the north-east of Key West, a massive obstruction, known as the American Shoal, having claimed the lives of more than a few unwary mariners, continued to threaten ships. Despite this, the obstacle was not marked until the 1870s, possibly because it was seen as an impossible task to build in such a place; instead of a light, brightly painted markers were placed on nearby Looe Key and directly over the shoal itself. Unfortunately, these proved of little use to seamen during the day and none at all at night. Encouraged by the success of other open-water construction projects, such as those at Sand Key and Alligator Reef, the Lighthouse Board finally decided to rise to the challenge and tackle the American Shoal. Backed by a Congressional appropriation of $75,000, construction of a lighthouse was underway by 1878.

Interestingly enough, the 109-ft iron-skeleton tower was not built on site, but rather in a mainland shipyard. It was then shipped to American Shoal in pieces and reassembled atop piles driven deep into the shoal and the underlying sea floor. Workrooms and living quarters for the station crew were built on a platform, held safely above the waves by the tower's sturdy legs, while the lantern room at the top held a first-order Fresnel lens.

Despite its costliness, it proved to be a first-rate facility. By the time the lighthouse had been completed and put into service in 1880, contractors had billed the government for about $125,000, which was half as much again as the original estimate. In spite of this, American Shoal can be regarded as an extraordinary bargain. Since 1880 it has guided mariners for more than 40,000 days and nights, bringing its average cost of construction down to little more than a paltry $3.00 a day.

The lighthouse lost its big prismatic lens after the station was automated in 1963, and its flashing signal is today produced by a modern optic. Power is supplied from batteries recharged by solar cells.

ST. MARKS LIGHT
St. Marks, Florida

Standing guard where land and water meet

It is a strange fact that some mainland lighthouses have proved far less durable than others built in the open sea. Often constructed on vulnerable sites, that are neither truly land nor water, many fell victim to erosion, some were knocked over by storms, and others were destroyed by fire or war.

An especially unlucky lighthouse was the one sited near St. Marks in the Florida Panhandle. Built in 1831, the original tower was so badly constructed that government inspectors rated it as little more than a haphazard pile of bricks and stone. It was torn down within months and was replaced by a second lighthouse, which although more sturdily built, was destined to last for only nine years. Undermined by rampant coastal erosion, it was demolished in 1840 and a third lighthouse was built on higher, safer ground. Two decades later the Civil War began and a company of Confederate raiders, having loaded the interior of the tower with gunpowder, blew it up to keep it from falling into Union hands.

Completed in 1867, the fourth St. Marks Lighthouse has endured for longer than any of its predecessors. The 82-ft conical brick tower rests on a massive limestone foundation, some 12ft thick; to help the tower to resist hurricane-force winds, it was given fortress-like walls more than 4ft thick – probably the reason why the tower still stands. The pristine marshes that surround the old lighthouse are now part of a wildlife preserve.

CAPE SAN BLAS LIGHT
Cape San Blas, Florida

Enduring despite misfortune

Another unfortunate light station marked Cape San Blas, the elbow of an L-shaped peninsula about halfway along the Florida Panhandle. Completed in 1847, the original lighthouse stood for only four years before being toppled by an exceptionally powerful hurricane. Swarms of mosquitoes then arrived to torment the crews attempting to build a replacement, spreading a deadly plague of yellow fever that delayed the project until 1856. Completed that year, the new tower stood for only a few months before another hurricane knocked it down. A third was burned down by Confederate troops during the Civil War,

and a fourth fell victim to erosion in 1882. There was an attempt to build a fifth, but the Lighthouse Service tender, bringing materials and supplies, sank before reaching the site

Given this catalog of woes, it is remarkable that a fifth Cape San Blas Lighthouse has managed to survive at all. But it had an innovative design, pioneered in the open waters of the keys, which has allowed this mainland light to serve mariners for more than a century. Completed in 1885, it has an iron-skeleton tower, that can be pulled apart and reassembled on safer ground whenever erosion threatens. The open walls of the tower offer little resistance

BELOW: As similarly unfortunate as the St. Marks Light, the Cape San Blas Light was plagued by disasters from the very first, including hurricanes, disease and war. The present lighthouse, the fifth in a chain dating back to 1847, was built in 1885, and its tower still stands.

to wind, allowing it to withstand even the fiercest hurricanes. Although the Cape San Blas beacon was discontinued in 1991, the old tower still stands.

CROOKED RIVER LIGHT
Carrabelle, Florida

An old skeleton tower that is stronger than hurricane-force winds

When hurricanes assail the Florida Panhandle, the brunt of their fury is usually borne by the long, narrow barrier islands, located a few miles from the mainland. Massive storms can actually change the shape of these islands or even wash them completely away. For many years, during the 19th century, a lighthouse on Dog Island guided lumber freighters into the small port of Carrabelle. Storm-driven tides, however, were constantly reshaping the island, necessitating the relocation of the station several times. Finally, an 1873 hurricane swept the lighthouse into the Gulf of Mexico, along with the keeper and his family.

During the aftermath, the Lighthouse Board wisely concluded that no lighthouse on Dog Island could withstand the forces of wind, tide, and erosion. To replace the Dog Island station, a new lighthouse was established on the mainland near the mouth of the Crooked river. The builders gave the lighthouse a similar treatment to that later used at Cape San Blas, giving it a heavily braced iron skeleton tower, designed to resist high winds. This has turned out to be the case, and the Crooked River Lighthouse has resisted dozens of major hurricanes and gales. What it could not resist, however, was the march of time and progress. Rendered obsolete by advanced buoyage and the introduction of new shipboard navigational systems, the light was finally extinguished in 1995. The big red tower still stands, however, and is occasionally opened to the public.

CAPE ST. GEORGE LIGHT
St. George Island, Florida

The Gulf of Mexico finally claimed its victim

Gulf-coast lighthouses have always been vulnerable to hurricanes and erosion, a fact of life that still pertains today. Built in 1852, the Cape St. George Light, near Apalachicola, survived to serve mariners for more than 150 years, despite being assaulted by countless storms. By the 1990s, however, the shifting coastal sands of the Gulf of Mexico had left the brick tower exposed to the tides, which

OPPOSITE PAGE: The builders of the Crooked River Light utilized a method similar to the one used at Cape San Blas, giving the lighthouse a heavily braced iron skeleton tower designed to resist high winds. It has since been rendered obsolete, but its red tower is occasionally opened to visitors.

LEFT: The Cape St. George Light unfortunately no longer exists. After many attempts to prop it up, it eventually fell into the sea in 2005, undermined by a series of heavy storms.

steadily undermined its foundations. The tower began to lean toward the waves, and structural engineers were of the opinion that it would collapse at any moment into the sea.

Florida preservationists struggled to save the historic building by removing sand and stone from the landward side of its sagging foundations, and by this method managed to straighten the leaning tower. Unfortunately, its reprieve held good for only a few years: blasted by a series of storms, during the fall of 2005, the old lighthouse finally subsided into the surf.

HILLSBORO INLET LIGHT
Pompano Beach, Florida

Centerpiece of the St. Louis World's Fair

FLORIDA

Atlantic Ocean

Hillsboro Beach

Coral Springs

Fort Lauderdale

Prone to erosion, and regularly bombarded by fierce hurricanes, it is practically impossible for masonry structures of any kind, particularly brick lighthouses, to survive in Florida. Therefore, many Florida lighthouses tend to be cast-iron or steel structures, similar to those at Sand Key or the American Shoal in the Florida Keys, or at Crooked River or Cape San Blas in the Florida Panhandle.

Among the tallest of Florida's iron-skeleton light towers is the one built at

OPPOSITE LEFT: Cape St. George Light.

LEFT: The Hillsboro Inlet Light is at 137ft one of the tallest of Florida's iron-skeleton towers. It was originally built in Chicago, where it featured in the 1904 St. Louis World's Fair. It was dismantled and reassembled at Pompano Beach a few years later.

FAR RIGHT: Port Boca Grande Light was built in 1890 in the style of a cottage on stilts, taking it beyond the reach of the tides. It once utilized an unusual 'Great Lakes' lens, which has since been replaced.

Hillsboro Inlet near Pompano Beach. Interestingly, the 137-ft all-metal tower was not actually built in Florida, but rather in a Chicago foundry, and its first duty station was not on the coast but at the 1904 St. Louis World's Fair. After it had dazzled millions at the great exhibition, the tower was pulled apart and shipped to Hillsboro Inlet, where it was reassembled and fitted with a second-order Fresnel lens.

The Hillsboro Inlet beacon has, since 1907, guided mariners hugging Florida's south-eastern coast or approaching Miami from the north. More than a century of service has not weakened the tower or dimmed its light, which is still focused using the original prismatic lens. The station's flashing white beacon has an extraordinary range of up to 28 miles.

PORT BOCA GRANDE LIGHT
Boca Grande, Florida

Standing beyond the reach of the flood tides

Iron stilts have helped more than a few Florida lighthouses to survive high tides and erosion, but not all such structures have been exceptionally tall. The relatively squat Port Boca Grande Lighthouse rests on iron stilts located just beyond the reach of the flood tides that wash under it during storms.

A square wooden cottage, with a small lantern perched on its roof, the lighthouse was completed in 1890. Threatened almost from the start by erosion, the lighthouse remained in use until the 1960s, when the waves of the Gulf of Mexico separated it from the mainland. Largely abandoned by the Coast Guard, the building fell into disrepair, but local lighthouse enthusiasts refused to let the old

lighthouse perish. Funds were raised to repair the building, and its light was returned to service in 1986.

The Port Boca Grande beacon was originally focused by a Fresnel lens of a type most often seen in the Great Lakes region. Slightly larger than a typical third-order lens, they are often referred to as 'third-and-a-half-order' or 'Great Lakes' lenses. This unusual article was removed when the station was deactivated, and today a fifth-order lens is housed in the tower.

Georgia

During the 1730s, General James Oglethorpe sought to establish a refuge in America for financially-bereft fellow Englishmen, who might otherwise have languished in debtors' prisons. Debt being no less a problem then than it is today, Oglethorpe had little difficulty in attracting settlers to the colony that came to be called Georgia, after King George II. Ships bringing new settlers and supplies, however, had great trouble navigating the mouth of the Savannah river to reach the colony's primary settlement near the present-day port of Savannah. To make the river entrance easier to find, Oglethorpe had a brick-and-cedar tower erected on Tybee Island. The 90-ft octagonal structure was one of the tallest buildings in America at the time, and although it had no light, the tower could be spotted during daylight hours from miles out in the Atlantic Ocean. The tower stood for several years before it became undermined by erosion and collapsed into the sea.

Oglethorpe and his Georgians built a second tower in 1742, but it, too, was soon threatened by erosion. A third tower replaced it during the 1770s, just as Georgia was about to be swept up into the American Revolution. At some point during this chaotic period, the new tower became a true lighthouse, when candles made of spermaceti, a waxy substance taken from the skulls of whales, were placed in a room at the top of the tower. At night the bright candle flames could be seen by vessels approaching the river channel.

Control of the Tybee Island Lighthouse passed to the new U.S. federal government in 1791, and over the next century, federal maritime authorities would order the construction of maritime towers at several other locations along the Georgia coast. Their beacons marked key inlets and the shores of the low, sandy barrier islands that separate Georgia's expansive marshlands from the open ocean. A few still perform the same function today, while others have succumbed to the destructive forces of wind, rain, fire, and time.

LIGHTHOUSES OF AMERICA

TYBEE ISLAND LIGHT
Near Savannah, Georgia

A mammoth tower hanging in the air

Mariners navigating the entrance to the Savannah river still look to Tybee Island for guidance, just as they have for the better part of three centuries. The island was marked with tall, unlit towers from 1733 until 1773, when Georgia's first true lighthouse was built. At first, its beacon was produced by spermaceti candles, and later by whale-oil lamps. During the 1850s, the station received a second-order Fresnel lens, but the tower and its almost priceless prismatic lens were destroyed by fire during the opening months of the Civil War. The conflagration was probably started by Confederate troops, determined to render the lighthouse useless to Union warships blockading Savannah itself.

After the war, the Tybee Island Lighthouse was rebuilt, using the lower walls of the old 1773 tower as a base. The new octagonal brick tower, completed in 1867, was of mammoth proportions. Soaring more than 150ft over the island sands, it was given massive walls at least 12ft thick, while a huge first-order Fresnel lens gave the station a beacon bright enough to reach ships more than 20 miles from the coast.

GEORGIA

Still active, the tower has a distinctive appearance. The upper third of the structure is painted black, while the middle third is white, making it seem as if it is hanging in the air when seen at a distance.

ST. SIMONS ISLAND LIGHT
St. Simons Island, Georgia

Haunted by the ghost of a former keeper

The Civil War was hard on lighthouses throughout the south, but especially so in Georgia. Like the Tybee Island Lighthouse, the 75-ft brick and coquina maritime tower, that had marked St. Simons Island since 1810, was also destroyed by Confederate troops as they retreated from the coast. Construction of a replacement tower got underway not long after the end of the war, but the project was interrupted repeatedly by outbreaks of a mysterious disease, likely to have been yellow fever or malaria. A new 104-ft brick tower and adjacent two-story Victorian-style keeper's residence was finally completed in 1872.

Painted white, the station's handsome tower remains an active aid to navigation. Its original third-order Fresnel lens still focuses the beacon, which can be seen from a distance of about 20 miles. The station's last keeper moved out of the attractive residence after the Coast Guard automated the light in 1953. Nowadays, the dwelling serves as a museum.

The St. Simons Lighthouse is one of many historic American towers, believed by some to house a resident ghost. In this case, the ghost is said to be that of a former keeper, killed by his assistant in a duel.

ILLINOIS

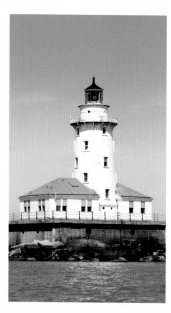

*N*o state or city owes more to the Great Lakes than Illinois and its mighty metropolis of Chicago. French explorers first reached the lakeshores of what is now Illinois in the 1760s and even then the commercial and strategic potential of the region was recognized. Located at the far south-western end of Lake Michigan, this part of the continental hinterland could be reached with relative ease by water. This made it a natural jumping-off point for settlers migrating towards the rich farm and ranchlands in the west. Raw materials and agricultural products could be loaded onto freighters here and shipped to markets in the east at a fraction of the cost of moving the same goods by wagon.

Chicago was indeed destined to become a major port and one of the world's great cities. As such, it needed maritime lights to guide lake freighters and passenger vessels into harbor. Chicago's first lighthouse was built in 1832, near to the mouth of the Chicago river, and other beacons would eventually follow. Most of the city's early maritime towers vanished long ago, and today, even their locations are not known with any certainty.

The lighthouse that marks Chicago's harbor today was built in 1893. At that time, a much more impressive lighthouse already existed at Evanston, Illinois, a few miles north of the city. Since nearly every vessel bound for Chicago approached from the north, the Grosse Point Light at Evanston was able to show them the way. Befitting its considerable importance, the Grosse Point station was assigned the most powerful lens and beacon anywhere on the Great Lakes.

GROSSE POINT LIGHT
Evanston, Illinois

Most powerful light on the Great Lakes

Rising several stories above the arching limbs of trees in a suburban lakeside neighborhood, north of Chicago, the graceful, cream-colored tower of the Grosse Point Lighthouse is ranked, by some, to be among the most beautiful buildings on the Great Lakes. Built in 1873, the lighthouse was intended to be superlative in every way. The 113-ft tower is the tallest masonry lighthouse on the lakes, and houses the Great Lakes' most powerful classic lens. Its hefty second-order Fresnel lens (there are no first-order lenses on the lakes) focuses a flashing beacon visible from many miles out in Lake Michigan.

Except for a few years during the Second World War, the station's bright beacon has guided vessels to Chicago and the harbor at Evanston for nearly 150 years. Completed only a few years after the Chicago Fire of 1871, the Grosse Point Light helped the great city to revive, by guiding ships bringing materials for the great task of reconstruction, and more importantly, by stimulating commerce. Now owned by the City of Evanston, the still-active light station is part of a popular museum complex.

LIGHTHOUSES OF AMERICA

The beautiful Grosse Point Light is situated in a quiet Chicago suburb. Its 113-ft tower focuses a flashing beacon that is visible for many miles out in Lake Michigan.

BELOW: Grosse Point Light.

FAR RIGHT: The cast-iron Chicago Harbor Light originally stood on land at the mouth of the Chicago river. In 1919, it was moved to the end of a breakwater, a mile out in Lake Michigan, where it could function more effectively.

CHICAGO HARBOR LIGHT
Chicago, Illinois

It illuminated the Columbian Exposition

Now located more than a mile out in Lake Michigan, the Chicago Harbor Lighthouse originally stood on land. The 82-ft cast-iron tower was built in 1893 on a site near to the mouth of the Chicago river. Then, in 1919 it was moved to the end of a recently completed breakwater, from where it could more easily guide vessels to safe harbor.

Like the tower itself, the station's original third-order Fresnel lens has had more than one home. When purchased from its European manufacturers, the lens was intended for the Point Loma Lighthouse, near San Diego, California. To promote good public relations, however, it was placed on display at Chicago's 1893 World Columbian Exposition. When the fair ended, federal maritime officials decided to leave the lens in Chicago and reassigned it to the city's recently completed harbor lighthouse. More than a century later, when the lens was finally removed from the harbor station and was replaced by a modern optic, it was shipped back to its original destination and is now on display at the Cabrillo National Monument at Point Loma.

INDIANA

*L*ike most other states bordering the Great Lakes, Indiana has benefited from the prosperity generated by ready access to water transportation. The area of Indiana bordering the lakes was once a soggy wilderness, but within a few generations it had evolved into one of the world's greatest industrial centers; iron, steel, petrochemical, and automobile assembly plants now line the 41-mile-long Lake Michigan shoreline. Yet for a state that is so closely linked to the lakes by commerce, it has very few lighthouses.

Ironically, the best-known and loved of Indiana's lighthouses is to be found in a place bearing the name of another state – Michigan City – where the excellent harbor has attracted commercial shipping since before the Civil War. Today freighters and pleasure craft entering the harbor are guided by an exceptionally attractive offshore pier lighthouse. During the 19th century, however, the city's maritime beacon was housed in a graceful Victorian structure, located on the mainland. Both lighthouses still stand, and both are ranked among the most historic buildings in Indiana.

ABOVE RIGHT: Michigan City Light, built in 1858, was basically a Victorian house with a lantern mounted on its roof. It was decommissioned in 1904 and is now a museum.

MICHIGAN CITY LIGHT
Michigan City, Indiana

She kept the light burning for 43 years

Michigan City's first lighthouse was, in essence, a Victorian house. What set it apart from other homes in the same neighborhood, however, was the small lantern perched on its roof. For more than 40 years the lantern housed a fifth-order Fresnel lens, which focused the beacon that guided vessels in and out of

the harbor. During nearly all that time, a single keeper tended the light. For the first three years after the lighthouse was built in 1858, its keeper was a man named John Clarkson. Then, in 1861, Harriet Colfax took over, refusing to relinquish the post until the station was deactivated in 1904. Of all the American lighthouse keepers, Harriet's 43-year career was one of the longest. After 1904, when the old Michigan City beacon and its venerable keeper were simultaneously retired, the former lighthouse continued for many years to serve as a residence for keepers tending the new pier light down on the harbor. Eventually, the old lighthouse was donated to the Michigan City Historical Society for use as a museum.

MICHIGAN CITY EAST PIER LIGHT
Michigan City, Indiana

Keepers seem to walk above the waves

A little after the turn of the 20th century, U.S. maritime authorities became convinced that a pier lighthouse would do a much better job of marking the harbor at Michigan City than the original lighthouse

located in the town. This was because experiments with similar pier light towers, in other states along the Great Lakes, had proved to be highly successful. The Michigan City East Pier

Light was ready for service in 1904, and its light has shone on all but a handful of nights ever since. Although the city's original lighthouse was decommissioned at that time, it continued to be used as the station residence until 1940.

Lake Michigan is frequently torn by gales liable to throw high waves against structures near to the shore, and may very well inundate a low, stone pier. To provide safe access to the tower, an elevated walkway runs the length of the pier, and to protect the lighthouse itself from damage, the tower has been wrapped in a cocoon of steel. Built on a square concrete platform, the tower rises approximately 50ft above the waters of the lake.

Michigan City East Pier Light was conceived as a more practical way of marking the harbor than the old Michigan City Light.

MAINE

MAINE

*D*uring the ice ages, glaciers as much as a mile thick grated, crushed and bulldozed the rocks of coastal Maine, before sliding off into the Atlantic Ocean. When the glaciers finally melted, about 10,000 years ago, they left behind a much altered landscape. The ice had sculpted ocean channels, penetrating up to 50 miles inland. Separating the channels were long, narrow fingers of land that pointed toward the open Atlantic, creating nearly 3,500 extra miles, crammed accordion-like into Maine's 228 miles of coast, and making it almost as extensive as that of California.

Another result is that Maine is now a veritable wonderland of lighthouses.

Maine has about 60 lighthouses, far more than any state other than Michigan. Many of these coastal sentinels remain active, guiding seamen and fishermen through some of the most treacherous waters on the planet. Some of Maine's beacons mark the seaward extremities of the craggy peninsulas left behind by the ice-age glaciers. Others guard the shores of the stony islands, that are scattered all along the coast, while still more point the way to coves and harbors in the vicinity of quaint towns and fishing villages, from Lubec in the east to Kittery in the west.

Maine is oriented east to west rather than north to south, which is why it is often described as 'downeast.' Here is a sample of the sturdy downeast lighthouses, along with details of their colorful histories.

PORTLAND HEAD LIGHT
South Portland, Maine

Some say this is the most beautiful lighthouse in the world

The Portland Head Lighthouse surely ranks among the most frequently photographed buildings in the world. Artists like it, too, and during the summer can be seen clambering over rocks with their easels, searching for just the right view. And no wonder: set against a background of wave-swept rocks, the venerable, white stone tower and handsome red-roofed keeper's dwelling are irresistibly picturesque. The lighthouse, however, was never meant to

be an objet d'art, or to inspire wonderment – it was meant to guide ships and save lives.

When the first U.S. Congress met after the ratification of the Constitution,

MAINE

OPPOSITE: *The Seguin Island Light was built on the orders of George Washington.*

BELOW: *The huge first-order Fresnel lense is still operational in Seguin Island's beacon today.*

the creation of a national lighthouse system was among its highest priorities. Indeed, one of the first projects undertaken by the new federal government was the lighthouse at Portland Head. Construction of the fieldstone tower had already begun, but had been brought to a halt after state and local sponsors ran out of money. Thanks to a small Congressional appropriation, work resumed in 1791, and the lighthouse was ready for duty late that year.

Except for a few minor breaks for repairs and renovations, the light has guided mariners ever since. When the Portland Head Light first went into service, George Washington was president, since when more than 40 presidents have led the nation over more than two centuries.

But compare this with the 20 keepers that have manned the light since 1791 until it was automated in 1989. In fact, for a period of nearly 60 years, beginning in 1869, the light was tended by members of a single family – by Joshua F. Strout and his son Joseph.

Today a modern optic produces the light signal that can be seen from a distance of 24 miles, but for more than a century, the station's light was focused by a large second-order Fresnel lens. When the last full-time keeper of the Portland Head retired in 1989, the big lens was removed and placed on display at a museum housed in the former station residence.

SEGUIN ISLAND LIGHT
Popham Beach, Maine

Its beacon remains focused by a grand first-order Fresnel lens

One of the most significant lighthouses along the coast of Maine, and probably along the entire eastern seaboard, is the one on Seguin Island, lying about two dozen miles east of Portland. The island lies just off the tip of a peninsula, extending seaward from the town of

Bath, the home of a major shipyard that builds U.S. Navy fighting ships.

The Seguin Island Light was established in 1795, only a few years after the Portland Head Light went into service. It was built by order of President George Washington, who more than likely had a hand in the appointment of its first keeper, a veteran of the Revolutionary War, called John Polersky. The old soldier's health was not equal to the assignment, however, and he was able to survive the hard work and harsh island climate for only six years. Perhaps not surprisingly, no one has stayed the course for long. From 1795 until the light was automated in 1985, nearly 100 keepers or assistant keepers have maintained the Seguin Island Light at one time or another.

Like Polersky, the original wooden lighthouse fell victim to the weather, collapsing in a storm in 1820. It was replaced by a sturdier stone structure, which lasted until 1857 when the existing 53-ft granite tower was completed. Remarkably, the huge first-order Fresnel lens, installed in the tower at that time, remains in the lantern room, where it still focuses the station's exceptionally powerful beacon; the lofty island provides much of the beacon's 180-ft elevation. In clear conditions, the light can be seen from dozens of miles out in the Atlantic Ocean.

WEST QUODDY HEAD LIGHT
Lubec, Maine

Dawn's earliest light strikes this historic tower

It is important to differentiate between West Quoddy Head Light, located in Quoddy Head State Park and overlooking the Bay of Fundy, and East Quoddy Head Light, located on the other side of the Lubec Channel, a constricted passage between Lubec and Campobello Island, which defines the border between the U.S. and Canada. What particularly distinguishes West Quoddy Head is that it marks the easternmost point in the United States; anyone present in the lantern room at dawn would be the first person in the United States to see the sunrise – unless, of course it is foggy. This part of the Maine coast is often shrouded in fog, which makes navigating its waters all the more perilous.

The West Quoddy Head Light and fog signal have been assisting mariners since 1808. Nowadays, both the light and fog signal are operated by automated timers and sensors, but until 1988 they were tended by resident keepers, who lived in a cozy dwelling beside the tower. As was the case at Seguin Island, the West Quoddy Head was generally a short-term assignment for keepers. Even so, a hardy Mainer, named Peter Godfrey, held the job from 1813 until 1837, a period of 24 years. One of the duties of early keepers was to fire the station cannon to alert

seamen when fog made the light all but invisible. Later, a 1,500-lb bell was used to produce the station's fog signal, and after that a steam-powered whistle. Today, when visibility is poor, West Quoddy Head uses an electric foghorn to warn mariners.

The red-and-white barrel-striped West Quoddy Head tower is a little under 50ft tall, but despite its relatively modest height, the station's flashing beacon can reach vessels up to 18 miles out at sea. The beacon is still focused by the same third-order Fresnel lens, placed here in 1858.

BASS HARBOR HEAD LIGHT
Mount Desert Island, Maine

Directs lobster boats near Acadia National Park

There are a cluster of historic maritime lighthouses in the vicinity of Mount Desert Island and Acadia National Park, located to the west of West Quoddy Head. Perhaps the best-known of these is the picturesque light station at Bass Harbor Head. As the name suggests, the station's light marks the

FAR LEFT & BELOW: The highly photogenic Bass Harbor Head Light, perched on its colored rocks, is one of a cluster of historic lighthouses located in the vicinity of Mount Desert and Acadia National Park.

produced by a slightly less powerful fifth-order Fresnel lens. The Bass Harbor Head beacon is red (for danger), although, interestingly enough, neither the electric lamps nor the lens itself are red. The light receives its color by passing through several red glass panels.

Automated in 1978, the station has no keeper, but Coast Guard personnel live and work here full-time, consequently, the interior of the lighthouse is not open to the public. Visitors are allowed to walk in the grounds, however, or follow a path down to the rocks.

GREAT DUCK ISLAND LIGHT

Near Frenchboro, Maine

Protects ships and rare seabird species

About five miles south of Bass Harbor, a sizeable, partially wooded island provides a safe haven for nesting eider ducks, petrels, and a variety of other rare seabirds. In fact, some believe that as much as 20 per cent of Maine's seabird population nests on this island. For fishermen and other mariners, however, the rocky shores of the island have never been considered a refuge, but rather a menace, especially when the Maine coast is locked in fog.

The Lighthouse Board placed a light and fog signal here in 1890, so that seamen would have a better chance of avoiding Great Duck's perilous rocks. Because the station was several miles from the mainland, and even further from the nearest town, keepers and their families had to be prepared to live in splendid isolation for most of the time. Mail and supplies were brought by boat, and when the Maine winter began to flex its muscles, deliveries were erratic to say the least. For years the island had a tiny school for the children of the keepers and their assistants.

The last keepers left Great Duck Island when the light was automated in 1986. At about the same time, the fifth-order Fresnel lens, that had served for nearly a century, was exchanged for a modern optic. Power for the light is now supplied by batteries recharged by solar panels. The Great Duck station displays a red light, that flashes once every five seconds.

PROSPECT HARBOR POINT LIGHT

Prospect Harbor, Maine

A friend to fishermen since 1870

The clean, unpolluted waters around Mount Desert Island and the Acadia National Park are teeming with fish and lobsters, of which commercial fishermen are only too aware. Coastal Mainers have been making a living from the sea for centuries, and hundreds of boats still put to sea each day to harvest the ocean's bounty. Most of those small but sturdy vessels sail in and out of small protective anchorages, similar to the one at Prospect Harbor, a few miles east of Mount Desert. The local fishermen and lobstermen have looked to the lighthouse for guidance since 1870, and the 38-ft white wooden tower has not

entrance to Bass Harbor, which, with its lobster pounds and bobbing lobster boats, attracts throngs of tourists during the summer months. More than a few of them also stop to visit the lighthouse, bringing their cameras with them. Like the older and grander Portland Head station, this gem of a lighthouse is exceptionally photogenic, and its image has been preserved in countless posters, art prints and photographs.

The colorful rocks on which the lighthouse stands also contribute to the overall picturesque scene – the same rocks that also reach out menacingly into the channel approaching Bass Harbor, which is, of course, why the light was sited here. The 32-ft brick tower and two-story wood-frame keeper's residence were built in 1858 and have changed very little over the years. The light signal is still focused by the fourth-order Fresnel lens, installed in 1902, but before then, the beacon was

LIGHTHOUSES OF AMERICA

OPPOSITE LEFT: Great Duck Island provides a safe haven for nesting eider ducks, petrels, and a variety of other rare seabirds. Mariners view the surrounding waters somewhat differently, especially when the island's coast is locked in fog.

FAR LEFT: Looking to the sea for their livelihood, Prospect Harbor Point Light has been guiding fishermen through waters rich in fish and lobsters for hundreds of years.

changed substantially in more than a century. The one exception is that its black cast-iron lantern no longer houses the station's original fifth-order Fresnel lens, and Prospect Harbor's flashing beacon is now produced by a modern optic.

Standing beside the tower is the handsome, wood-frame residence, sited here in 1891. No keeper has lived in the house since the light was automated in 1934, but it is now used as a guest cottage for military personnel visiting the nearby naval base.

BURNT COAT HARBOR LIGHT
Swan's Island, Maine

A 19th-century lighthouse serving an 18th-century fishing village

During the summer months, ferries make a daily run, carrying adventurous vacationers to Swan's Island. Once there, however, they may be shocked to find that there are few tourist amenities. Swan's Island is primarily a fishing community, as it has been for centuries. The island's chief anchorage is Burnt Coat Harbor, which is stacked with lobster pots and colorful buoys.

The narrow entrance to the harbor has never been easy to navigate, and until

the 1870s the fisherman of Swan's Island had no light to guide them into port. In 1872 the Lighthouse Board ordered construction of a pair of light towers, on Hockamock Head near to the harbor entrance, which turned out to be more confusing than helpful; some claimed they caused more wrecks than they prevented. To solve this problem, the smaller of the towers was removed in 1885. The remaining 47-ft tower still stands, and its light remains in service.

It is said that Burnt Coat Harbor was named after a soldier in the Revolutionary War who, sickened by the violence, took refuge on Swan's Island. Rather than change sides and become a turncoat, his protest against the conflict was to symbolically burn his uniform.

ISLE AU HAUT LIGHT
Isle au Haut, Maine

Champlain's 'High Island' has only one red light

Most of Acadia National Park is located on Mount Desert Island, but a

OPPOSITE: Prospect Harbor Point Light.

BELOW: Swan's Island has few amenities for tourists, but a ferry still operates, bringing visitors to the island to view Burnt Coat Harbor Lighthouse and the nearby 18th-century fishing village.

FAR RIGHT: Although predominantly a fishing community, Isle au Haut still attracts its fair share of vacationers in summer. But while its light tower is still in use, and has been guiding fishing boats for the last 100 years, the keeper's residence is now an unusual bed-and-breakfast inn.

substantial portion of this rocky, wave-swept vacationers' paradise extends over onto Isle au Haut. A rugged, largely pristine island some 20 miles from the mainland, Isle au Haut is sparsely populated; during the summer months, however, it attracts its share of determined hikers, although most of the hardy souls who live here all the year round are fishermen.

To ensure that island fishing boats would return safely from sea, the government established a maritime light here in 1907, and it has remained in service ever since. The station consists of a keeper's house and a 48-ft granite-and-brick tower, standing on rocks at the edge of the tides.

While the light tower is still in use, the lovely old residence no longer houses keepers and their families. Rather, it is home to one of Maine's most unusual and remote bed-and-breakfast inns. Visitors cannot fail to enjoy its warm, homely atmosphere, where the food is praised by all fortunate enough to have sampled it.

Isle au Haut received its name from no less a person than Samuel de Champlain, when he was exploring these coasts in 1604, having sighted its forested hills on the horizon. He also named the adjacent island, its name having been anglicized to Mount Desert.

SADDLEBACK LEDGE LIGHT
Penobscot Bay, Maine

A lonely outpost, besieged by the Atlantic Ocean and suicidal ducks

BELOW: Saddleback Ledge rises unexpectedly from the waves, near to the middle of Penobscot Bay's busy east channel. But for the Saddleback Ledge Light, that has marked the spot since 1839, vessels seeking to enter the Penobscot river would have been faced with certain disaster.

About midway along the Maine coast, the Penobscot river flows into a broad bay that is more than 30-miles-wide at its mouth. Rich in fish, lobsters and seabirds, Penobscot Bay is home to a myriad of islands. Some of these, such as Deer Island, Vinalhaven, and the 10-

MAINE

mile-long Islesboro, are relatively large and dotted with summer homes and fishing villages, while others are mere specks of rock, pounded by waves. Saddleback Ledge is of the latter variety, but it is of no less concern to mariners, despite its small size.

Nearly impossible to see from the water, Saddleback Ledge rises unexpectedly from the waves, near to the middle of the bay's busy east channel. But for the reliable maritime light and fog signal, sited here in 1839, vessels moving through the channel toward the entrance of the Penobscot river would have been faced with certain disaster.

Since Saddleback Ledge was so isolated from the nearest community, keepers had to live on the completely barren rock all the time. Theirs was not an enviable assignment, as the ledge was under constant siege by waves and threatened by storms. On one occasion, shortly before the Second World War, the lighthouse even came under attack from birds. In a bizarre incident, reminiscent of Alfred Hitchcock's film, *The Birds*, based on the novel by Daphne du Maurier, an enormous flock of wild duck and geese targeted

Saddleback Ledge, and throughout one evening flew en masse into the lantern, breaking windows and cracking the station's Fresnel lens.

Much to the relief of its keepers, no doubt, the light was automated in 1954, since when the keeper's residence, the oil house, and other station structures have been washed away by the tides. The 42-ft granite tower remains, however, and its flashing beacon continues to warn mariners of the imminent danger.

EAGLE ISLAND LIGHT
Eagle Island, Maine

An isolated lighthouse with an errant fog bell

In 1839, the year the Saddleback Ledge Light was also completed, a similar structure was built on nearby Eagle Island. Unlike Saddleback Ledge, however, Eagle Island was not barren, but its keepers were nonetheless isolated. The nearest towns were separated from the island by miles of rough water, and the island itself was difficult to approach by boat. Even today, the best way to see this historic light station is from the air.

Only 30-ft-tall, the Eagle Island tower is shorter than that of nearby Saddleback Ledge; however, it stands near the edge of a rocky cliff that adds to the elevation and effectiveness of its beacon, the extra height placing the light more than 100ft above the waves. The fourth-order Fresnel lens, that had served here for nearly a century, was removed after the station was automated during the early 1960s. When the Coast Guard tried to move the 1,200-lb brass fog bell, it broke away, rolled down a steep slope, and fell into the ocean. Later, it was salvaged by a lobster fisherman and sold to a local artist, who used it as a dinner bell.

DICE HEAD LIGHT
Castine, Maine

Guards a 17th-century village that once flew four flags

For many years, the most important beacon in Penobscot Bay was that of the Dice Head Lighthouse, situated on a lofty promontory about halfway between the open Atlantic and the mouth of the Penobscot river. The light marked not only the busy central portion of the commercial shipping channel, but also the harbor entrance of Castine, one of the oldest and most historic communities in North America. Founded by fur traders during the early

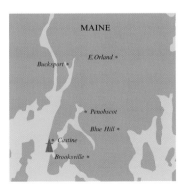

The Eagle Island Light.

1600s, the town was fought over for centuries and, at one time or another, was ruled by four different nations – France, Holland, Britain, and the United States. Many battles were fought in or near Castine, and in one of these, a hero of the Revolutionary War, Paul Revere, led an unsuccessful attack on a British fort that dominated the heights above the town.

Those same heights would later give the Dice Head beacon a tremendous boost, making it visible from as much as 17 miles out in the bay. Established in 1829, the light emanated from atop a 51-ft, cone-shaped tower, but much of its impressive elevation came from the hillside on which it stood. Keepers lived in a Cape Cod-style residence and reached the tower by way of a short, covered passageway, offering some protection from Maine's bracing winter weather. The last keepers left Castine when the station was deactivated in 1956. At that time, an automated light was placed on a skeleton tower, located at the foot of the hill below the station. In 1999, a fire severely damaged the keeper's residence, which has since been restored.

FORT POINT LIGHT
Stockton Springs, Maine

Points the way to lumberjack country

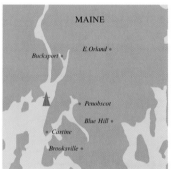

LIGHTHOUSES OF AMERICA

Like the old stone tower at Castine, the Fort Point Lighthouse, on the opposite side of Penobscot Bay, stands on high ground. For this reason, its light can reach vessels far out in the bay without the assistance of a tall tower. Since 1857, the station has been utilizing a fourth-order Fresnel lens, which focuses a beacon visible from distances of up to 15 miles. The lighthouse itself dates from 1836, but the original stone tower was replaced by the existing square, brick structure in 1857.

The Fort Point Light marks the entrance to the Penobscot river, once a vital shipping route for transporting the lumber, produced in great quantities by sawmills in Maine's backcountry forests. Even today, freighters moving up and down the river depend on Fort Point's beacon for guidance. Perhaps more important than the station's light, however, is its foghorn, which, in conditions of poor visibility, sounds an audible warning every 10 seconds.

Although no longer used today, a pyramid-shaped structure, one of the last of its kind, and still standing adjacent to the lighthouse, houses a fog bell. Also in the vicinity is Fort Pownall, where British and American troops fought a key battle during the Revolutionary War.

OPPOSITE & ABOVE: Fort Point Light stands on high ground, making it very visible despite the squatness of its tower. The pyramid structure, one of the last of its kind, supports a fog bell that is no longer in use.

CURTIS ISLAND LIGHT
Camden, Maine

This village light still guides windjammers

With its mountain and ocean vistas, cozy inns, and delightful restaurants, the picturesque village of Camden, on the western shores of Penobscot Bay, is a great place for a summer getaway. Visitors love to stroll down by the harbor, where the tall masts of visiting schooners give the place a distinctly 19th-century atmosphere. The only thing missing from the nautical scene is a lighthouse – or so it would seem. But Camden does in fact have an historic lighthouse, even though it cannot be seen from the village waterfront. It is located on the far side of a small, forested island, situated near to the harbor entrance.

The Curtis Island Light was established in 1836, at about the same time that the original lighthouse at Fort Point was built. The squat 25-ft tower, that serves Camden today, dates to 1895. The fourth-order Fresnel lens, that has been housed in the tower for nearly a century, was removed in 1994, and is now on display in the Camden Public Library. The Curtis Island beacon remains in service, but its green light is now produced by a modern optic.

ROCKLAND BREAKWATER LIGHT
Rockland, Maine

Located at the end of an artificial peninsula

As its name suggests, Rockland is a town with a hard edge to its past. During the 19th century, countless tons of stone, quarried in the nearby mountains, were shipped from Rockland to markets in Boston, New York and beyond. This made Rockland a busy commercial port, but unfortunately for the captains of freighters, its harbor was exposed to high waves thrown against the coast by the rolling Penobscot Bay. To quieten the harbor waters, the government built a massive breakwater in 1888, which was extended to a length of more than a mile in 1902. To prevent ships' pilots from losing sight of the low breakwater, and crashing into it, a lighthouse was built at the breakwater's outer end.

The Rockland Breakwater Lighthouse consists of a 25-ft brick tower, a brick fog-signal building, and an attached one-and-a-half-story keeper's residence. The dwelling is attached to both of the other structures, making it easier for the keeper to tend

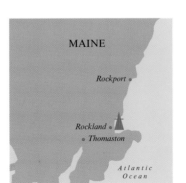

FAR LEFT: Camden's historic Curtis Island Light is situated a little away from the town, on a small island near to the harbor entrance.

the lighthouse equipment. The dwelling has ceased to be inhabited since the light and fog signal were automated in 1964, both of which remain in operation. The fourth-order Fresnel lens, installed when the station was built, has been replaced by a modern optic. It produces a flashing beacon visible from distances of up to 17 miles.

Rockland is home to the Shore Village Museum, devoted largely to lighthouse equipment and memorabilia. Of special interest here is the museum's substantial collection of lenses. Museum staff are on hand to answer questions concerning lighthouse engineering and technology, and can give an insight into the lives of lighthouse keepers and their families.

OWLS HEAD LIGHT
Rockland, Maine

Guided cold stone freighters and frozen lovers

Near to the entrance of Rockland Harbor lies an unusual rock formation, that some say bears a resemblance to an owl, known as Owls Head. It has been the location of the Owls Head Lighthouse since 1826, which has clung to the rocks here for more than 180 years. Its fixed white beacon marks not only the entrance to the harbor, but also the outer western rim of Penobscot Bay. The station's beacon, visible from up to

OPPOSITE: Rockland Breakwater Light sits atop a massive breakwater, built in 1888 to calm the waters in the harbor. Like many lighthouses today, the keeper's quarters now house a maritime museum.

BELOW: The Owls Head Light has been clinging to an unusual rock formation, near the entrance to Rockland Harbor, since 1826.

MAINE

RIGHT & OPPOSITE: Marshall Point Light offers a safe haven to mariners entering the tiny fishing village of Port Clyde.

16 miles out at sea, is focused by the same fourth-order Fresnel lens placed here in 1856.

Over the years, the keepers at Owls Head have accumulated a wealth of amazing stories, such as that of the so-called 'frozen lovers.' It is said that a seaman and his love were caught in a blizzard aboard a deserted schooner, at anchor in Rockland Harbor. The high winds broke the schooner's anchor chain, blowing the vessel against Owls Head, where the young lovers were driven onto the deck by rising waters. They were soon covered in a thick coating of ice, but the keeper discovered the hapless couple and was able to thaw them out, allowing them to be married soon after. Another story tells of a dog, whose ceaseless barking saved a fog-bound freighter. The dog had supposedly been trained to pull the fog-bell's rope whenever fog descended.

MARSHALL POINT LIGHT
Port Clyde, Maine

Nellie's little lighthouse

One of Maine's many long, narrow, finger-like projections reaches its seaward tip just beyond the tiny fishing village of Port Clyde, at a place called

BELOW RIGHT & OPPOSITE:

BELOW RIGHT & OPPOSITE:
Permaquid Point Light was built in
1827 to warn vessels of the treacherous
rocks in the vicinity. Its short, sturdy
tower allows it to withstand the
punishing Atlantic gales that frequently
batter the point.

Marshall Point and, like many other
such peninsulas, it is marked by a
lighthouse. The beacon marks the point
and helps to guide fishing boats and
other vessels to Port Clyde, a delightfully
quaint place, where lobster pots are
stacked in front of nearly every house.
Visitors usually end up at the nearby
Marshall Point Museum, which exhibits
memorabilia taken from lighthouses all
along the Maine coast. One of the most
interesting things, however, is the
museum building itself, in that the two-
story colonial-revival structure was once
the residence of the keeper of Marshall
Point himself.

Marshall Point's 30-ft tower is
located a short distance from the
museum, standing on an outcrop of rock
at the water's edge. Like several of
Maine's smaller light towers, it consists
of a modest brick cylinder, built atop a
massive granite base. The black iron
lantern now holds a modern optic,
producing a fixed white light visible for
seven miles. The fifth-order Fresnel lens,
that served here from 1858 until the light
was automated in 1980, was removed
and placed in the Shore Village Museum
in Rockland. The Marshall Point
Lighthouse is featured in a children's
book called *Nellie the Lighthouse Dog.*

MATINICUS ROCK LIGHT
Matinicus Island, Maine

Caught in the grip of an angry sea

Many of the best lighthouse stories are
about the day-to-day struggles of keepers
and their families. One such dramatic
tale is attached to the Matinicus Rock
Lighthouse, located on a barren island
many miles from the mainland. Here, in
1856, a teenage girl named Abbie
Burgess, managed to save several
members of her family and a pet chicken
from the ravages of a howling Atlantic

storm. Young Abbie hurried everyone
into the sturdiest of the station's two
stone towers, just as a giant wave was
about to break over the island. The wave
carried off the Burgess residence and
several other buildings, but left the tower
and its survivors unharmed. Afterwards,
in a letter to a friend on the mainland,
Abbie wrote matter-of-factly of the
incident: 'You have often expressed a
desire to view the sea out on the ocean
when it was angry. Had you been here on
19 January [the day of the storm], I
surmise you would have been satisfied.'

During the 19th and early 20th centuries, the Matinicus Rock station displayed two lights, emanating from two separate towers to ensure that seamen recognized the signal in time to avoid running aground. The first towers, sited here in 1827, were built of wood and, not surprisingly, quickly deteriorated. They were replaced in 1848 by stone towers that were better able to withstand the island's harsh conditions.

These towers stood up well to the weather, but following the great storm of 1856, they were replaced by even stronger granite structures. Each of the new towers was large enough to accommodate a third-order Fresnel lens. During the 1920s, the Lighthouse Service decided to discontinue one of the lights, leaving the other in operation. It remains in service, but today houses a modern optic, rather than the Fresnel lens it had for more than a century.

PEMAQUID POINT LIGHT
Damariscotta, Maine

Looks down on waves of stone

MAINE

Wicasset

New Harbor

Permaquid Point

Newagen

Atlantic Ocean

Ice-age glacial abrasion and the pounding of ocean waves have so scarred the rocks at Pemaquid Point that they have taken on fantastical shapes, thought by some to resemble ocean waves that have been turned to stone. Over the years, more than a few seamen have found these rocks far from romantic, and a good deal harder than they look. Pemaquid Point has claimed more than its share of vessels, which have either been forced onto the rocks or blown off-course by storms. The navigational light established here in 1827 helped to reduce the losses and continues to warn mariners today, just as it has for more than 180 years.

The 38-ft stone tower has thick walls, which it has needed to survive the ravages of the gales that strike the area almost every year. Not all of the station's original structures have been quite so durable, however, and the fog-signal building and engine house were mortally damaged by a rare New England hurricane in 1991. The tower still holds the station's 150-year-old fourth-order Fresnel lens, using it to focus a flashing beacon visible for up to 15 miles out at sea.

FAR LEFT & BELOW: Permaquid Point Light is famous for the strange, wave-like appearance of its rocks, produced by ancient glaciation and the action of the tides.

FAR RIGHT & OPPOSITE: There used to be two light towers at Cape Elizabeth, but today only one beacon is in use. The other tower is now a private residence, as is the former keeper's dwelling.

CAPE ELIZABETH LIGHT
Cape Elizabeth, Maine

Two lights that are now one of a kind

Originally known as Two Lights, the Cape Elizabeth Lighthouse was one of several light stations, located along the east coast, that guided mariners with twin beacons. Cape Elizabeth was unusual in that one of its towers displayed a fixed light, while the other had a flashing light. This unusual arrangement made it easy to distinguish the Cape Elizabeth light signal from others along the coast. Like multiple-light stations elsewhere in the United States, this was converted to a single-light beacon during the 1920s.

Established in 1811, the Cape Elizabeth station consisted of a residence for the keeper and a pair of 65-ft rubblestone towers, spaced about 300ft apart. The entire facility was completed by contractors at a cost of under $5,000, but the structures were nonetheless sturdy, despite their bargain price. They lasted for more than half a century, in fact, right up until the 1870s, when they were replaced by the impressive cast-iron towers seen at Cape Elizabeth today. Only the tower on the eastern side of the complex remains in

service today. The other is privately owned, as is the former keeper's residence. The second-order Fresnel lens, once housed in the east tower, was removed in 1994 and put on display in the Cape Elizabeth Town Hall. Today, a modern optic produces the station's beacon; in clear weather, its flashing white light can be seen for up to 15 miles out at sea.

CAPE NEDDICK LIGHT
York, Maine

Mystery faces stare out from island rocks

There are some who say that the face of Abraham Lincoln is visible in the rocks of the Nubble, a small craggy island just off Cape Neddick, a few miles east of the Maine/New Hampshire border. Others say the rocks bear the likenesses of shipwrecked victims or of ancient mariners lost at sea. Chiseled out and

eroded by eons of exposure to wind and waves, the island rock formations do indeed suggest faces, but who they belong to is known only by people with vivid imaginations.

Given its name by passing fishermen, the Nubble possesses something rather more important than strange rocks – in fact an historic lighthouse. During the late 1870s, the Lighthouse Board ordered construction of a lighthouse at Cape Neddick to guide vessels headed eastward toward Portland, Maine, or westward toward Portsmouth, New Hampshire. Completed in 1879, the Cape Neddick Light consists of a two-story, wood-frame keeper's residence, connected to a 40-ft cast-iron tower by a short passageway. These, and the other 19th-century structures, remain in excellent condition. The blinking red light of Cape Neddick's beacon is still focused by the station's original fourth-order Fresnel lens.

OPPOSITE & BELOW: The Cape Neddick Light stands on a craggy outcrop, known as the Nubble, situated just off the cape. It was completed in 1879, and remains in excellent condition.

An interesting architectural feature of this well-preserved 19th-century lighthouse, is the iron railing around the gallery at the top of the tower, decorated with small cast-iron lighthouses. During the Christmas season, families drive in from as far away as Boston to enjoy the spectacle of the strings of colorful lights, that have been used to decorate the entire station.

MARYLAND

MARYLAND

*M*uch like Maine, *Maryland has far more shoreline than one might expect, given the relatively modest size of the state. Encompassing only 9,800 square miles, and with less than a quarter of the land area of neighboring Virginia, Maryland is only a little larger than Massachusetts. Maryland has a relatively short sea coast, yet this small mid-Atlantic state can boast a shoreline nearly as long as California's. Some 3,190 miles of Maryland actually touches water, and most of that considerable distance is accumulated as the state wraps itself around Chesapeake Bay.*

More than 200-miles-long and up to 30-miles-wide, the Chesapeake is the collective estuary of the Susquehanna, Potomac, James, and about 150 other rivers and streams. The waters are alive with game fish and some of the most delectable crabs on the planet.

Chesapeake Bay is no less historic than America itself, in that a controversy over control of Chesapeake's navigation led to the framing of the U.S. Constitution. During the War of 1812, a British fleet sailed into the bay on its way to attack Fort McHenry and Baltimore. The attack was repulsed, but the treacherous waters of the bay almost certainly claimed more British fighting ships than the ineffective cannon of the American defenders. It was also in the Chesapeake that the Civil War ironclads, Virginia *and* Monitor, *fought their famous and ultimately inconclusive duel.*

Littered with shoals and shifting sandbanks, Chesapeake is notoriously difficult to navigate, and has ensnared and destroyed far more than its share of ships and smaller vessels. So it comes as no surprise that Chesapeake's Maryland shores should be home to some of America's oldest and most historic lighthouses.

CONCORD POINT LIGHT
Havre de Grace, Maryland

Tended by a single family for nearly a century

With a conical stone tower that is only 32ft tall, the Concord Point Lighthouse may be small, but it has a mighty history. Built in 1827 by a Maryland journeyman contractor, John Donohoo, the little tower has cast its light over the waters of upper Chesapeake Bay for more than 180 years.

Despite nearly two centuries of intensive use and exposure to the damp Chesapeake climate, the structure has required few major renovations or

repairs, which is remarkable when one thinks that its cost to the government was only $3,500.

For nearly a century the Concord Light was kept by one or another member of the O'Neil family. The first keeper was John O'Neil, a widely celebrated hero of the War of 1812. In 1838, he passed the job on to his son, John Jr., who maintained the beacon until he died in 1863. His wife, Esther, then kept the light burning until 1878, when her son, Henry, took over the job; when the station was automated in 1920, Henry O'Neil's son, Harry, was in charge of the light.

In 1975, the Coast Guard decided that the Concord beacon was no longer necessary and the old light was deactivated. The lighthouse was restored by local preservationists some years later, and its beacon was brought back into service as a private aid to navigation. The fixed green light is focused by a fifth-order Fresnel lens.

COVE POINT LIGHT
Solomons, Maryland

Built at a bargain price, it has guided ships for more than 180 years

Another of John Donohoo's Maryland lighthouses has guarded the entrance to the Patuxent river since 1828. Like the much smaller Concord Point tower, the

51-ft brick tower of the Cove Point Lighthouse has required few repairs and looks very much today as it did during the 1820s. Interestingly, the tower cost the government even less than the one at Havre de Grace and, at $2,300, also included the price of the land.

For many years, the station's beacon was produced by a lamp, fueled by whale oil with a reflector system, which eventually gave way to a kerosene lamp and a lens optic. The fourth-order Fresnel lens, installed in 1987, remains in service today.

Chesapeake Bay is notorious for its frequent dense fogs; for many years, keepers were obliged to stay awake when it was foggy so that they could ring the station bell. The old bell still hangs above the fog-signal building, which today houses a modern, electrically-powered foghorn.

OPPOSITE RIGHT BELOW: The Concord Point Light is located at the point where the Susquehanna river meets the tidal flow of Chesapeake Bay, creating waters that are hazardous to navigate.

BELOW: Cove Point Light was built in 1828 to meet the needs of mariners traveling south down Chesapeake Bay en route to the Patuxent river.

MARYLAND

PINEY POINT LIGHT
Valley Lee, Maryland

Lighthouse of the presidents

Yet another historic John Donohoo lighthouse can be seen at Piney Point, near to the mouth of the Potomac river, and although no longer in active service, the old tower remains in excellent condition. It is now part of a six-acre park and museum complex, devoted largely to the history of the lighthouse and of lower Maryland. The history of Piney Point is closely linked with that of the U.S. presidency: just as Camp David is now used as a presidential retreat, Piney Point once served as a cool summer residence for several 19th- and early-20th-century presidents, including James Madison, James Monroe, Millard Fillmore, Franklin Pierce and Theodore Roosevelt.

Built in 1836, the Piney Point Lighthouse was for many years among the most important beacons on Chesapeake Bay; it marked a key turning-point for vessels entering the Potomac and heading toward Washington, D.C. and the terminus of the Chesapeake & Ohio Canal. However, river traffic grew increasingly lighter after the canal shut down in 1924, and the lighthouse itself was finally put into retirement in 1964.

HOOPER STRAIT LIGHT
St. Michaels, Maryland

This cottage-style lighthouse was cut in half and moved ashore

Because the serpentine channels of Chesapeake Bay could not always be adequately marked by maritime lights located on the shore, a completely new type of lighthouse was spawned. Known

as cottage-style or screw-pile lighthouses, they were built directly over shoals or at important turning-points located far from the mainland. Most consisted of a small hexagonal or octagonal wooden building, with a modest tower rising through its roof. Usually, they rested on iron piles that had been painstakingly driven or screwed into the thick mud beneath the shallow waters of the bay. These structures were relatively inexpensive, and by the late 19th century, as many as 45 of them marked Chesapeake and

OPPOSITE LEFT: Piney Point was built by John Donohoo, who also built the Concord and Cove Point Lights. No longer operational, it is now the chief attraction of Piney Point Lighthouse Park.

BELOW: The Hooper Strait Light was originally built in 1879, located at the top of Tangier Sound in upper Chesapeake Bay. The lighthouse was decommissioned in 1966 and was moved to the Chesapeake Bay Maritime Museum at St. Michaels.

MARYLAND

ABOVE: The keeper's accommodation at the Hooper Strait Light.

FAR RIGHT: Drum Point Light was decommissioned in 1962. It was moved up the Patuxent river to the Calvert Marine Museum at Solomons in March 1975, where, with advice from the daughter of the last keeper, it was restored to its former glory.

several of its tributary rivers and inlets.

All but a few of Chesapeake's cottage-style lighthouses have now disappeared, but several can still be seen, and two of them now serve as attractions of the well-known Maryland coastal museums. One is the Hooper Strait Lighthouse, now located in St. Michaels, where it continues to delight visitors who come to the Chesapeake Maritime Museum throughout the year.

The 41-ft six-sided structure, that was completed in 1879, once stood in the open waters of the Hooper Strait, in upper Chesapeake Bay, until it was retired in the 1960s. In 1967, the

building was cut in half and taken by barge to St. Michaels, where it was reassembled and put on display. Still fitted with its classic Fresnel lens, it serves as a reminder of Maryland's extraordinarily rich maritime heritage.

DRUM POINT LIGHT
Solomons, Maryland

The Patuxent veteran now teaches history

The Calvert Maritime Museum, in Solomons, on Maryland's south-western Chesapeake shore, is home to a fascinating collection of historic ships

and nautical artifacts. Among its finest examples is a lighthouse, complete with its furnished living quarters and Fresnel lens. For more than 90 years, the Drum Point Lighthouse stood near the mouth of the Patuxent river. Built in 1883, it was decommissioned in 1962, and about a dozen years later was moved upriver to Solomons.

One of the least expensive of the Chesapeake lighthouses, the Drum Point residence and tower was built at a cost to the government of only $5,000, despite which it survived nearly 80 years of active service. Now handsomely restored, it continues to serve a worthwhile purpose by reminding the American people of their nautical history.

SEVEN FOOT KNOLL LIGHT
Baltimore, Maryland

The bright-red sentinel continues to welcome visitors

The cottage-style Chesapeake towers were by no means the first lighthouses to be built on piles in open water. During the 1850s, the Lighthouse Board experimented with many innovative lighthouse designs and construction

techniques. Completed in 1855, the Seven Foot Knoll Lighthouse consisted of a round building, with a small, cylindrical tower set atop its flat roof. Painted bright red, the structure made a bold statement during the day, while at night its powerful beacon warned vessels away from the treacherous shoal on which it stood.

Seven Foot Knoll's sturdy piles held it safely above the tides for more than 130 years until the Coast Guard deactivated it in 1987. The following year, the 220-ton building was moved to its present location in the popular Baltimore Inner Harbor district, where it now serves as a tourist attraction.

FAR LEFT: The Seven Foot Knoll Light originally stood in open water at the entrance to the Patapsco river, Chesapeake Bay. In 1988, the lighthouse was moved to Baltimore's Inner Harbor, where it is now part of the Baltimore Maritime Museum.

MASSACHUSETTS

*F*ew are likely to argue that Massachusetts is the cradle of both American democracy and of the national lighthouse system. North America's very first lighthouse was erected on an island near the entrance to Boston Harbor in 1716, while the second, in what was now the United States, was completed in 1746 at Brant Point on Nantucket Island. Several other Massachusetts lighthouses were also built and commissioned during the 18th century, including Plymouth in 1769, Cape Ann in 1771, Baker's Island in 1798, Cape Cod, also in 1798, and Gay Head, on Martha's Vineyard, in 1799. All of these coastal beacons went into service either before or during the lifetime of George Washington, and many other names would be added to the long list of Massachusetts maritime lights during the early 1800s.

Massachusetts's close affinity with lighthouses is hardly surprising, since it was founded by mariners and has always played a vital role in American maritime commerce. Since the 1600s, ships have been crowding into Boston Harbor, and visiting fishing and whaling ports on Cape Cod, Nantucket, Martha's Vineyard, and the Massachusetts mainland. Over the centuries more than a few lost their way and become wrecked on uncharted shoals or else they simply vanished into the vastness of the Atlantic Ocean. Although the lighthouses were built to prevent such tragedies and save lives, the beacons were also intended to stimulate trade, which they did, to an extent that shocked business and government leaders on both sides of the Atlantic.

It was, in fact, an incident directly related to maritime trade that was to change American history. On 16 December 1773, a party of anti-tax political activists marched down to the Boston wharves, boarded a freighter, that no doubt had been guided into port by the Boston Lighthouse, and dumped its cargo of tea into the sea. Perhaps to add a touch of humor to an otherwise serious act, the raiders dressed as Mohawk Indians. However, the joke was lost on the British authorities, who ordered a blockade of Boston Harbor; this was the first in a sequence of events that led to the Revolutionary War and independence for 13 of Britain's former colonies. Among the victims of the war, ironically enough, was the original Boston Lighthouse, that was blown up by British troops as they evacuated Boston in 1775.

BOSTON LIGHT
Boston, Massachusetts

North America's oldest and most historic maritime light

Established in 1716, on a barren island near the entrance to what was then America's busiest and most prosperous port, the Boston Lighthouse is the oldest maritime light station in North America. The cost of building the 70-ft rough stone tower, and of keeping its candles lit, was paid by means of a tax on ships entering the harbor. The first keeper of the Boston Light, a man named George Worthylake, earned only £50 a year for lighting the candles each and every evening and snuffing them out at dawn. After only a year on the job, Worthylake was killed when his small boat was overturned in the harbor.

Destroyed during the Revolutionary War, the lighthouse was rebuilt in 1783;

the rubblestone tower that was completed at that time still stands, after more than two centuries of exposure to the harsh New England climate. Knowing the lighthouse would constantly be pummeled by gales, the stonemasons gave the tower stout walls, nearly 7ft thick at the base. During the 1850s, the tower was raised by 15ft and its walls were lined with brick.

LIGHTHOUSES OF AMERICA

Although the old tower is still an important seamark, much of its value today lies in its extraordinary historical significance. Not only was it America's first lighthouse, it was the nation's last official lighthouse to have a full-time keeper. Even today, coastguardsmen still live in the old residence beside the tower, although the light itself, that was not fully automated until 1999, is monitored and controlled by computers. Still focused by the hefty second-order Fresnel lens, installed in 1859, the station's beacon can reach vessels up to 20 miles out at sea. It could be truly said that it has been seen and noted in the logs of more sea captains than any other light in America.

BRANT POINT LIGHT
Nantucket, Massachusetts

Welcomes tourist-laden ferries to Nantucket

Ferry passengers approaching the island of Nantucket are greeted by the winking red light of one of the oldest and most historic lighthouses in America. The first lighthouse to mark Brant Point, and the harbor of Nantucket, was completed in 1746, only 30 years after the Boston Lighthouse first went into commission.

LEFT: America's first lighthouse, the Boston Light is situated on Little Brewster Island in Boston's outer harbor. The original tower was built in 1716, but was destroyed during the Revolutionary War. It was rebuilt in 1783.

OPPOSITE RIGHT BELOW: The Boston Light's second-order Fresnel lens.

It was built for £200, much of the money provided by whalers, who were disturbed at the frequency with which ships ran aground in the sandy shallows.

The new light improved navigation and helped to increase the fortunes of local whaling captains, but the little lighthouse itself, being a wooden structure, did not fare as well as the mariners it served, and was burned to the ground after only a few years. Its replacement was also destroyed by fire, and over the two-and-a-half centuries since its service began, at least eight Brant Point towers have gone up in flames or been bowled over by storms. The current 26-ft tower has stood the longest, in fact, since 1901.

CAPE ANN LIGHT
Thatcher Island, near Rockport, Massachusetts

One of its keepers was a staunch Tory during the Revolutionary War

Another colonial lighthouse marks Thatcher Island, a rocky obstacle lying off the end of the peninsula that forms the northern lip of Massachusetts Bay. The Cape Ann Light was unusual among early lighthouses in that it

OPPOSITE: Brant Point Light is located on Nantucket Island. It was first built in 1746, since when it has had many reincarnations, the present lighthouse dating from 1901. It was automated in 1965, and is still in operation. It was added to the National Register of Historic Places in October 1987.

LEFT: The Cape Ann Light Station, originally dating from colonial times, comprises two massive towers. They stand on rocky Thatcher Island, which is a hazardous obstacle to shipping, a mile off the coast of Rockport. It was probably the first station to mark a danger spot rather than an entrance to a harbor.

ABOVE: The twin towers of the Cape Ann Light Station.

FAR RIGHT: The first Cape Cod Highland Light was built in 1798 to warn of the presence of dangerous sand bars, lying about a mile to the northeast, known as the Peaked Hill Bars. The present lighthouse, dating from the 1850s, had to be moved to a safer distance away from the edge, when rapid erosion of the bluffs threatened to undermine the tower and cause it to collapse into the sea.

displayed two lights rather than one. The station's twin towers were completed in 1771, only a few years before the opening shots of the Revolutionary War were fired at Concord, about 40 miles to the west. The Cape Ann Lighthouse was inevitably caught up in the conflict, when the then keeper of the light, an outspoken Tory named James Kirkwood, began to condemn the revolutionary fervor that was sweeping the colonies during the mid-1770s; his opinions were to cost him his job.

Extinguished soon after Kirkwood was fired, the lamps atop the twin towers were not relit until after Massachusetts and the other colonies had secured their independence. The new keeper, who took over in 1784, was a man named Samuel Huston, and over the next two centuries, more than 60 names would be added to the list.

The two 124-ft granite towers, seen on Thatcher Island today, were not built in colonial times. Somewhat ironically, they replaced the original structures in

1861, just before the outbreak of another mighty conflict, the American Civil War. These massive structures have withstood countless powerful storms and remain in remarkably good condition, although only the southernmost of the two is still operating. The lamp and lens in the north tower were removed almost a century ago, when the government decided to discontinue use of multi-light maritime beacons. The existing light flashes red every five seconds and can be seen from a distance of about 17 miles.

CAPE COD (HIGHLAND) LIGHT
Truro, Massachusetts

Cape Cod's oldest and most famous beacon

Although Cape Cod is such a prominent geographical feature that it supposedly can be seen from space, it is quite difficult to see it from the surface of the

MASSACHUSETTS

Provincetown

Atlantic Ocean

Truro

Wellfleet

Cape Cod Bay

South Wellfleet

North Eastham

Eastham

ocean. Bisecting some of the most heavily congested shipping channels in the world, the Cape's tawny bluffs rise up unexpectedly from the waves and, from a distance, look more like low-lying cloud banks than land. For this reason, thousands of vessels, large and small, have ended their days buried in the Cape Cod sands.

During the late 1700s, when the fledgling United States government began to mark prominent points up and down the Atlantic coast, the first and most important of these new light stations was the one built on the north-eastern rim of Cape Cod in 1798.

The original Cape Cod tower was made of wood and stood only 45ft tall. There was no necessity for it to be any taller, since the bluff already gave it a substantial boost, placing it more than 150ft above the Atlantic Ocean. Later, the wooden tower was replaced by a brick structure, which served until 1857, when it was superseded by a 66-ft brick tower with a cast-iron lantern. The latter structure can be seen at Truro today, though not on its original site.

The Cape Cod bluffs were created by the interaction of wind and water on sands deposited during the last ice age, and rapid erosion is now destroying them. When the existing lighthouse was

The multicolored cliffs, on which the Gay Head Light now stands, raises it to a height of more then 170ft above the waves. The first tower was erected here in 1799, and would eventually be described as the ninth most important coastal light in America. In 1854, a first-order Fresnel lens, that had previously been exhibited at the World's Fair in Paris, was obtained. Two years later a new lighthouse was built to house the lens, which contained 1,008 prisms.

built during the 1850s, it stood more than 500ft from the edge of the bluffs, but by the 1990s, the eroding cliffs were less than 100ft away and the foundations of the historic tower were now under considerable threat. In 1997, a $1.5-million preservation project saved the old lighthouse, by having it loaded onto rails and moved a safer distance from the cliffs. Today the station still alerts mariners with its flashing white light, which can be seen for up to 23 miles.

GAY HEAD LIGHT
Martha's Vineyard, Massachusetts

Stands atop a rainbow-colored cliff

Gay Head Lighthouse was built on a site similar to that of the Cape Cod tower, and at about the same time. It was given its rather interesting name because of its rainbow-colored cliffs, which also provided an excellent location for a lighthouse, since they contributed to the beacon's elevation. Although the barrel-shaped Gay Head tower is only 51ft tall, its light shines out over the water from a height of more than 170ft.

The existing tower is not the original. An octagonal wooden tower was erected here in 1799, during the administration of John Quincey Adams,

America's second president. It served until 1856, when it was replaced by the brick structure seen here today. The station once had several buildings, including a keeper's residence and an oil storage facility, but they were demolished by the Coast Guard after the light was automated in 1960.

Nowadays, the lonely Gay Head tower is a popular destination for tourists flocking to Martha's Vineyard during the summer. The area is also popular with pleasure boaters and other mariners, who watch for the lighthouse's alternating red-and-white beacon, which can be seen from a distance of 25 miles.

MARBLEHEAD LIGHT
Salem, Massachusetts

This steel giant withstood New England's most destructive hurricane

Nowadays, vessels are guided into Salem's harbor by a lighthouse that is unlike any other on the Massachusetts coast. At Marblehead, in 1895, near the harbor entrance, government contractors erected a giant steel skeleton. Consisting of a narrow metal cylinder, held in place by eight, heavily-braced steel legs, the tower was designed to resist storm-force winds. Because it had no walls, the wind was able to pass through it, placing very little pressure on the structure.

The skeleton tower replaced a more conventional lighthouse, built here in 1846. This rather squat building served its purpose well enough, but by the late 19th century, clusters of summer cottages were being built at Marblehead which began to obscure the station's beacon. This fate is unlikely to befall Marblehead's existing steel tower, which soars to a height of 105ft.

Marblehead's wind-resistant design was put to the test in 1938, when a

vicious hurricane descended on New England. The structure proved to be well up to the challenge, but at the height of the storm, electrical power was lost all along the coast. To keep his light in operation, Marblehead's keeper, Harry Marden, ran a cable down to his car so that he could use its battery as a source of power.

FORT PICKERING LIGHT
Salem, Massachusetts

Stands beside the walls of a ruined fort

From its position facing the giant iron skeleton at Marblehead, on the opposite side of the Salem harbor entrance,

THIS PAGE: The diminutive Fort Pickering Light once faced the giant Marblehead Light across Salem harbor. From 1871 until 1969, when it was replaced by a buoy, it was a help to mariners making their way into Salem harbor, who would line up the Fort Pickering and Derby Wharf Lights after passing Baker's Island.

OPPOSITE: The Derby Wharf Light sits at the entrance of Salem harbor – once a bustling port. Although only 23ft tall, it served its purpose faithfully from 1871 to 1977. In response to a campaign by preservationists, however, its light was restored and the lighthouse was reactivated in 1983.

Pickering Lighthouse seems particularly diminutive by comparison. Built in 1871, this cast-iron midget is only 32ft tall, and while the structure itself may be unimpressive, the station's light has long been a welcome sight to the pilots of vessels entering Salem harbor.

The station served mariners for nearly a century before its beacon was replaced by a buoy in 1969. Local lighthouse enthusiasts and preservationists, however, were able to restore the little tower in 1983, and today its light shines forth once more. Fort Pickering's red beacon can be seen from about four miles out in the harbor.

DERBY WHARF LIGHT
Salem, Massachusetts

Guided China tea clippers to Salem

Blocky and squat, the Derby Wharf Lighthouse is hardly impressive, as light towers go, but the little building, and the nearby Salem waterfront, share a fascinating history, for Salem was once one of America's busiest and most prosperous ports. During the 18th and 19th centuries, fortunes were being made by captains of the China tea clippers. These sailed in and out of Salem harbor, carrying large cargoes, not only of tea, but also of silks, spices, and fine chinaware, from expeditions to Asia's Far East that could take anything up to five years to complete.

Over the years, a number of maritime lights were established to guide these large vessels, and a host of other shipping also began to find its way into the harbor. After 1870, ships were guided to the Salem docks by a tiny lighthouse at the end of a massive commercial facility, known as Derby Wharf. The wharf was named for the man who built it, Elias Derby, who is believed to have been America's first true millionaire.

Although only 23ft tall, the little Derby Wharf Lighthouse served its purpose faithfully, remaining in operation until 1977. By this time, Salem was no longer seeing the volume of commercial maritime activity that had caused the lighthouse to be built during the 19th century; however, it is now a magnet for tourists, and most visitors enjoy a walk out to the lighthouse. To celebrate Salem's rich history, city preservationists have rekindled the Derby Wharf Light and it shines today just as it did in days gone by, its flashing red light visible from a distance of about six miles.

EASTERN POINT LIGHT
Gloucester, Massachusetts

Best friend of Gloucester fishermen

Where Salem once accommodated clippers, bringing tea and other precious commodities from China, nearby Gloucester attracted mariners of a different kind, who sought their fortunes closer to home.

Gloucester is essentially a fishing port, and its fishing fleet burgeoned during the early 1800s. In 1832, the government built a lighthouse to guide the fleet and its rich Atlantic harvest into harbor. The first lighthouse consisted of

OPPOSITE & LEFT: The Eastern Point Light stands on a rocky peninsula that acts as a natural breakwater to calm the waters of Gloucester harbor. It is particularly important to fisherman, who follow its guiding light, seen for nearly 25 miles from out in the Atlantic.

FAR RIGHT: Chatham is the site of Cape Cod's second lighthouse. After the completion of the Highland Light, the placing of another lighthouse on the cape's south-eastern tip was the obvious next step. In 1808, to distinguish it from the Highland Light, the Chatham station was given twin lights, which could be lined up to mark the safe channel away from shifting sand bars. These wooden structures were replaced by brick towers in 1841, but due to erosion, they had fallen into the sea by 1877, after which they were replaced by metal towers lined with brick. During the 1920s, the Lighthouse Service discontinued all of its multi-beacon light stations, including the one at Chatham. In 1923, the north tower was moved to Nauset Beach, about 15 miles away.

a modest stone tower, erected on Eastern Point, a craggy peninsula forming a natural breakwater near the harbor entrance. It was replaced with a more substantial structure in 1848, but the 36-ft brick tower seen today was built in 1890, its tower linked to the two-story keeper's dwelling by a covered passage; this was not considered a luxury on the Massachusetts coast, where icy blizzards are capable of freezing a man's blood.

Like most other light stations established during the 19th century, it once utilized whale-oil lamps, with reflectors to intensify the light, but the tower was eventually equipped with a fourth-order Fresnel lens. The highly polished crystal lens was removed in 1994 and replaced by a modern lighting apparatus, and while it may be lacking in historic merit, the new optic is most effective. Fishing boats and other vessels follow its flashing signal from up to two dozen miles out in the Atlantic.

CHATHAM LIGHT
Chatham, Massachusetts

Its twin towers fell over a cliff

The Cape Cod (Highland) Lighthouse first displayed its light in 1798, but while its beacon was of considerable assistance to mariners, it guarded only a dozen or so miles of beach. During the early 19th century, as vessels large and small continued to run aground and be torn apart by the cape's crushing surf, it became obvious that Cape Cod needed additional lighthouses.

Cape Cod's second maritime light was established in 1808 at Chatham, about 40 miles south of Truro's Highland Lighthouse. This enabled mariners, sailing along the cape's outer arm, to keep one or other of the lights in view at all times. To make it easier for seamen to distinguish between the lights, and from

others along the Massachusetts coast, the Chatham station was given a twin beacon. Its lights emanated from a pair of octagonal wooden towers, positioned atop a bluff that added elevation to the beacons. The wooden structures were replaced by brick towers in 1841.

Chatham's brick towers served for more than 30 years, but by the 1870s they were facing the same peril that would threaten the Highland Light during the 1990s: the cliffs were rapidly eroding away. Each year more and more of the crumbling bluff began to fall away, disappearing into the ocean. By 1877, nothing remained to support the lighthouse and both of its towers tumbled over into the sea. Later that same year, the Lighthouse Board had a pair of cast-iron towers, fitted with high-quality fourth-order Fresnel lenses, sited at Chatham. Constructed of riveted iron plates, much like the hull of a ship, Chatham's all-metal towers were highly resistant to wind and rain, having an added advantage in that, whenever the eroding cliff-edge came too close, the towers could be relocated.

During the 1920s, the Lighthouse Service discontinued all its multi-beacon light stations, including the one at Chatham. In 1923, the north tower was moved to Nauset Beach, about 15 miles

MASSACHUSETTS

up the coast. The south tower was left at Chatham, where it continues to operate its powerful flashing beacon.

NAUSET BEACH LIGHT
Nauset Beach, Massachusetts

Once the home of the famed Nauset Sisters

Nauset Beach was once the site of what was probably the most unusual light station ever to have marked the American coast. It displayed not one or two, but three separate lights, operating from three separate towers located about 100ft apart. The towers were all less than 30ft tall, but they stood on a high bluff, and the three-light arrangement made for a particularly effective seamark. Built by contractor Winslow Lewis in 1838, the original Three Sisters were made of brick. They were replaced in 1892 by wooden towers, which served until 1911 when erosion forced the Lighthouse Service to shut them down. In 1923, the Sisters were replaced by a single cast-iron tower, brought to Nauset Beach from the former twin-light station at Chatham.

Many years later, the iron tower would itself be threatened by erosion, and by 1990, the 90-ton metal cylinder

was teetering on the edge of the cliffs. To save the historic structure, the National Park Service had it moved a short distance inland. The NPS now owns the still-active Nauset Beach Lighthouse, along with the wooden Three Sisters towers, now located in a small park a short distance from Nauset Beach.

Compared with the Boston Light, the Graves Lighthouse is a relative newcomer. In fact it is Massachusetts' youngest lighthouse, even though its weatherbeaten appearance would indicate to the contrary. It was built in 1905 to mark dangerous ledges, that lurked beneath the waters of Boston Harbor. Known as 'graves,' these ledges were named for Rear Admiral Thomas Graves, who came to America from London in 1628 and was an early settler in the area.

GRAVES LIGHT
Boston, Massachusetts

The big Graves lens now brightens the Smithsonian

Once, long ago, the Boston Light was the only maritime beacon in Massachusetts or, for that matter, the entire North American continent. Over the centuries, since the colonial tower was first built in 1716, it has been joined by many other coastal sentinels.

Today, in fact, it is only one of several guiding lights in Boston Harbor. Just north of the Boston Lighthouse, for instance, stands a gray, weather-streaked stone tower, that looks for all the world like a part of the local geology, as if it arose out of the ocean

thousands of years ago. This is the Graves Light, built on ledges (graves) in the channel, and although it looks very old, it dates only to the early 20th century. To put the relative youth of the Graves Light into perspective, it should

be remembered that when the tower was completed in 1905, the Boston Light had already served mariners for more than 180 years.

It took two years to build the 113-ft tower, with its massive, interlocking granite blocks, out in open water. The building was designed to resist the high winds and waves of mighty sea storms, and this it has achieved for more than a century. At least three generations of keepers have relied on the tower's structural resilience to preserve their very lives, for their entire time was spent, living in cramped quarters inside the 30ft-wide stone cylinder. The last keeper left the station in 1976, when the light was automated.

Nowadays, the flashing Graves beacon is generated by a modern optic,

but until only a few years ago, its light signal was focused by a huge first-order Fresnel lens. Consisting of a metal frame and more than a ton of polished glass prisms, the big lens was removed and is now on display at the Washington, D.C. Smithsonian Institution.

MINOTS LEDGE LIGHT
Cohasset, Massachusetts

Lover's Light was once a watery coffin

One of the greatest tragedies in lighthouse history occurred in April 1851 at Minot's Ledge. The previous year, an experimental iron-skeleton tower, that was believed to be more than a match for the most powerful of gales, was sited on a ledge, just off Cohasset. This proved false, however, when little more than a year after the station's whale-oil lamps had been put into service, a mighty storm, coming from the north-east, bore down on the Massachusetts coast. Two assistant keepers were on duty at the time, and being unable to reach the shore, they decided to ride out the storm. As the waves mounted higher and higher, however, the metal structure of the tower began to fail. Finally, it collapsed into the sea, killing the young keepers,

who are believed to have kept the light burning to the very last.

It was nearly a decade before the fallen lighthouse was replaced, but the granite tower, also built atop the ledge in 1860, still stands, the tower rising 97ft above the open waters of Massachusetts Bay. Having been exposed to high winds and pounding waves for more than 150 years, it remains in remarkably good condition. Its massive blocks, some of them weighing more than two tons, interlock in such a way that the pressure, exerted on the structure by the ocean, strengthens rather than weakens the walls.

Standing guard over one of the Atlantic coast's most notorious obstacles, Minot's Ledge Light has saved the lives of hundreds, perhaps thousands of mariners. Unlike many lighthouse beacons nowadays, it is still considered vital to safe navigation, and seamen striving to avoid the dangerous ledge, watch for the station's unusual signal, which warns them with a series of quick flashes, grouped in a one-four-three sequence. To local romantics, this suggests the phrase, I/L-O-V-E/Y-O-U, and has led to Minot's Ledge being nicknamed 'The Lover's Light.'

NOBSKA LIGHT
Woods Hole, Massachusetts

Guards a bank of perilous shoals

Summer tourists, crossing back and forth by ferry from Martha's Vineyard, are comforted on seeing the flashing beacon of the Nobska Lighthouse, which has warned mariners of the presence of dangerous shoals for the better part of two centuries. Established in 1829, the original light station consisted of a modest stone cottage with a small lantern perched on its roof. Today, the beacon shines from an octagonal metal lantern room, set atop a

CENTER LEFT: Minot's Ledge Light is the second tower to have marked these treacherous rocks. During a fierce storm in April 1851, the first lighthouse collapsed into the sea, killing two of its keepers. The present granite tower, built to replace it in 1860, still guards the ledge, its tower rising 97ft above the open waters of Massachusetts Bay.

40-ft cylindrical steel tower. Built in a distant shipyard, and brought to the site in sections, the tower was assembled by bolting together curved iron plates.

Unlike many lighthouses nowadays, Nobska still houses a Fresnel lens, its polished glass prisms having focused the station's beacon since 1888. The light flashes white every six seconds and can be seen from a distance of about 13 miles. The Nobska Lighthouse is located near Woods Hole, home of a famous ocean research center.

SCITUATE LIGHT
Scituate, Massachusetts

A darkened sentinel is rekindled after 130 years

Established near Scituate in 1811, the light station was intended to guide vessels into the town's small harbor and to warn of the presence of the dangerous ledges, that were lurking offshore.

The Scituate station performed the first task admirably, but not the second. With dismaying regularity, the hulls of vessels, large and small, continued to be ripped open on the ledges, more often than not with tragic results. The continuing loss of ships, crews,

passengers, and valuable cargoes prompted the establishment of an offshore light, constructed in open water directly over Minot's Ledge, the most destructive of the obstacles. This rendered the Scituate Light obsolete, and it was boarded up in 1860.

But the Scituate Light was destined to have another chapter added to its story. Having somehow survived more than a century of disuse and neglect, the tower was acquired by the town of Scituate and restored as a local

attraction. Then, in 1991, more than 130 years after its beacon last shone, it was returned to service as a private aid to navigation, its light flashing white every ten seconds.

The Scituate tower has certainly been worth preserving: although built little more than 20 years after the framing of the U.S. Constitution, the structure has a surprisingly modern look, its inwardly-sloping octagonal walls lending it a sleek, almost rocket-like appearance.

OPPOSITE: The Nobska (Nobsque) Light is located at the south-western tip of Cape Cod, between Buzzard's Bay and Vineyard Sound. The original structure was a design common at the time, being a lantern room installed on the roof of a residence, but it was too heavy and caused the light's roof to leak. The present Nobska Light dates from 1876 and is made of steel. It still has a Fresnel lens, which beams a white light. The light was automated in 1985.

BELOW LEFT: Dating from 1811, the Scituate Light's main purpose was to warn ships away from the treacherous ledges outside its harbor. Mariners, however, complained that its beacon was not high enough to be seen in time to take avoiding action, so another 15ft was added to its tower in 1827. The construction of the new Minot's Ledge Light led to the Scituate Light being deactivated in 1860. In 1991, however, it was restored to its former glory as a local attraction and is now a private aid to navigation.

MICHIGAN

*M*ichigan predominates as the Great Lakes State: its shores are washed by Erie, Huron, Michigan and Superior, in short, by every one of the Great Lakes apart from Lake Ontario. Michigan is divided into a Lower and an Upper Peninsula: both have extensive lakeside frontages, and there is a lake view, or at least the promise of one, from practically any point in the state. In fact, in Michigan, it is impossible to be more than 100 miles from one or another of the Great Lakes.

Michigan has 3,000 miles of shoreline, nearly half as much again as New York, Pennsylvania, Ohio, Indiana, Illinois, Wisconsin and Minnesota, all put together; many lighthouses were therefore needed to mark so many miles of Michigan's shore, and over the years, the government has established more than 100 navigational beacons, which is more than any other state, including Maine, with upwards of 70, Florida, with approximately 50, and California, with about 40. Many of Michigan's historic lighthouses remain in operation and all are revered for the contributions they have made to the safety and prosperity of the Midwest and of the nation as a whole.

Despite the lights that shine toward the lakes from nearly every Michigan port and prominent headland, vessels large and small are still being lost along these shores. Some of these wreckings have been especially tragic and, like that of the Edmund Fitzgerald, *in 1975, make for dramatic reportage. Shipwrecks are nearly always noteworthy, but averted tragedies never make it into the newspapers or the history books. No one will ever know how many ships and lives have been saved by Michigan lighthouses, or how many potential victims made it safely to port, helped by beacons guiding them from the Michigan shore.*

Brick cylinders, steel skeletons, cast-iron barrels, square concrete monoliths, and wood-frame residences with towers attached – nearly every type of lighthouse can be found in Michigan – and some that are rarely seen elsewhere. Range beacons, arranged one behind the other to help navigators keep to a narrow, safe channel, were first used in Michigan. Usually built on stone piers, extending far out into the water, range lighthouses are graceful in appearance during the day and make attractive displays at night. In fact, some of Michigan's range lights are so beautiful and historic that they have found their way onto postage stamps.

ST. JOSEPH PIER LIGHTS
St. Joseph, Michigan

Its towers grace a U.S. postage stamp

Having once seen the St. Joseph Inner and Outer Pier Lighthouses, nearly everyone ranks them among the most beautiful maritime towers in America. They have been the subject of films, paintings, murals, and postage stamps, not to mention countless photographs. Part of what makes this light station so attractive and interesting is the fact that there are two towers rather than one, and they are connected by an elevated walkway which is brightly lit at night. The St. Joseph Pier Lights are range beacons, which means that the lights have been positioned to align with one another when seen from the middle of the channel leading to the harbor entrance; the lights appear to tilt to one side or the other when a vessel begins to deviate from its mid-channel course.

A more conventional lighthouse, built in 1832, once marked St. Joseph's harbor, but it was deactivated and demolished not long after the existing pier lights were established in 1907. Located near the end of the pier, the outer tower is a cylindrical, cast-iron structure, while the 57-ft inner tower,

LIGHTHOUSES OF AMERICA

The St. Joseph Pier Lights present such a pretty picture that they are often used as subjects by artists and photographers, and have even been featured on postage stamps. Their more serious purpose, however, is to guide vessels safely into harbor. These are range beacons, in that the lights have been positioned to align with one another when seen from the middle of the channel; whenever a vessel begins to deviate from its correct mid-channel course, the lights appear to tilt to one side or the other.

located closer to the shore, is taller. The top of the tower is octagonal in shape and rises from the roof of the station's fog-signal building.

WHITEFISH POINT LIGHT
Paradise, Michigan

Home of a popular shipwreck museum

The steel tower and wooden residence at Whitefish Point, on Michigan's Upper Peninsula, is famous for several reasons, not the least of which is the association of this strategically placed maritime beacon with a number of notorious shipwrecks, including the case of the SS *Edmund Fitzgerald*. In November 1975, the steamship was proceeding eastward during a howling blizzard, when she mysteriously vanished about 20 miles north of Whitefish Point. The Whitefish beacon should have been the last thing the doomed crew saw, but unfortunately it was not, for on the night in question, the beacon had been put out of action by the storm.

Recognizing the dangers associated with this part of Lake Superior, government maritime officials established a major light station at Whitefish Point in 1848. The stone tower, built here at that time, soon proved itself to be no match for the

FAR LEFT: The dangerous waters around Whitefish Point, and the numerous tragic shipwrecks that had occurred in the vicinity, led to the establishment of the Whitefish Point Light in 1848. In 1862, the stone tower was found to be unequal to the apalling weather conditions in Michigan's Upper Peninsula, and was replaced by an iron skeleton tower, similar to those found in Florida. The light still stands, pointing the way towards the locks at Sault Ste. Marie.

horrendous weather in the Upper Peninsula, and the storms that frequently blew in off Lake Superior.

In 1862, therefore, it was replaced by an iron skeleton-tower, of a type pioneered in the Florida Keys. Braced by iron legs, and with a network of cables and supports, its central steel cylinder housed a staircase leading to the lantern room, some 75ft above the lake. With no solid walls to catch the wind, the tower was designed to withstand even the worst blizzards, and it has succeeded in doing so for nearly 160 years. The light remains in operation, shepherding vessels into the calmer waters of Whitefish Bay and directing them towards the locks at Sault Ste. Marie. The historic two-story keeper's residence, and other station buildings, now house fascinating exhibits connected with the wreck of the *Fitzgerald* and many other Great Lakes shipping disasters.

POINTE AUX BARQUES LIGHT
Port Austin, Michigan

Little Boats Point

Several of Michigan's best-known lighthouses mark prominent headlands that define large, commercially significant bays. This is the case with the Whitefish Point Light and Whitefish Bay and also with the Pointe Aux Barques Light, located near the entrance of Saginaw Bay on Lake Huron. Saginaw Bay was frequented by mariners as long ago as the early 18th century, when French fur traders came here to purchase furs culled by various Native American tribes. It was the French who gave Pointe Aux Barques (Little Boats Point) its name.

During the 19th century, Saginaw Bay began to attract all types of shipping, and in 1848 the government

established a light at Pointe Aux Barques to help sailors safely navigate the entrance. The light proved ineffective, and in 1857 the original tower was replaced by the 89-ft brick structure that still dominates the point today. Some consider it among the finest and most attractive light towers on the Great Lakes. The third-order Fresnel lens, placed here in 1857, has since been replaced by a modern optic.

GRAND TRAVERSE LIGHT
North Port, Michigan

A museum that resembles an early-20th-century light station

Another Michigan beacon, that once marked the entrance to a large bay, was

FAR LEFT: The Pointe Aux Barques Light is located near the entrance to Saginaw Bay on Lake Huron, an important shipping route. Dating back to 1848, it is still operational today, but now has a modern optic operating its beacon.

the shoals. The beacon, and the polished glass prismatic lens producing it, remain in operation. It is of an unusual type, slightly larger than an ordinary third-order Fresnel lens. Often used in light stations in the Midwest, lenses like these are sometimes referred to as 3.5-order or Great Lakes lenses. Now in the care of a local historical society, the residence and other station buildings are home to a popular museum.

OPPOSITE & LEFT: Although Grand Traverse Light was deactivated during the 1970s, it remains in excellent condition, and its keeper's dwelling and attached tower are now used as a museum.

BELOW: Sturgeon Point's powerful beacon still warns shipping of the presence of dangerous shoals, but the residence now houses a museum.

the Grand Traverse Light. For many years, it guarded Lake Michigan from the end of a long, narrow peninsula, reaching northward from Traverse City. The beacon operated from a lighthouse located on Cat Head Point, but during the 1970s, the task of guiding vessels into the bay was transferred to an automated light, mounted on a steel tower. Although its light no longer shines, the old lighthouse remains in excellent condition. The two-story brick-built keeper's dwelling, and attached tower, are now used as a museum, and period furnishings and artifacts heighten its resemblance to a typical, early-20th-century light station.

STURGEON POINT LIGHT
Harrisville, Michigan

Guards a notorious Lake Huron reef

While some Michigan lighthouses existed to mark bays or prominent

headlands, others were intended to indicate the presence of dangerous shoals. The rocks and reefs just west of Harrisville, on Lake Huron, have claimed many vessels. To warn ships away from these hazardous obstacles, the Lighthouse Board established a light at Sturgeon Point in 1870. The station's 71-ft conical brick tower was fitted with a powerful Fresnel lens, able to reach vessels long before they ran aground on

MICHIGAN

Keeps Lincoln's light burning

President Abraham Lincoln, himself a Midwesterner, ordered the construction of the new lighthouse at Presque Isle, even though it would not be completed until long after his assassination in 1865. Finally completed in 1871, the station was impressive: its 113-ft brick tower was one of the tallest on the lakes and its third-order Fresnel lens among the most powerful in the Midwest. The big lens remains in use, focusing a light signal visible for up to 25 miles out in Lake Huron. The lighthouse property is now part of a beautiful lakeside park, owned and maintained by the Presque Isle township.

BIG SABLE POINT LIGHT
Ludington, Michigan

Protected from the weather by a suit of armor

The north-south trend of Michigan's western shore is broken by a pair of sweeping capes, that extend for several miles out into Lake Michigan. They are known as Big Sable and Little Sable

Old Presque Isle Light (above) was built to warn Lake Huron shipping of the need to turn north-west towards the safe passage that led to the Sraits of Mackinac and Lake Michigan. Its beacon was not quite powerful enough for the task, however, and President Lincoln ordered a taller tower to be built, that was completed in 1871. This is known as the New Presque Isle Light (see opposite right).

OLD PRESQUE ISLE LIGHT
Presque Isle, Michigan

A resident ghost climbs the stairs to the tower

The Great Lakes follow many twists and turns, that require vessels to make frequent changes of course. Key turning points are often marked by beacons, like the one on Presque Isle, near to where navigators on Lake Huron must begin to steer toward the north-west, so that the locks at Sault Ste. Marie or the Straits of Mackinac, leading to Lake Michigan, can be safely reached.

A stone lighthouse, built here in 1840, was intended to alert passing vessels to the need for a change of course, but its beacon was never strong enough to handle the important task. Consequently, a much taller tower was built on Presque

Isle in 1871 and was fitted with a more powerful optic. The original lighthouse still stands, but is now used as a museum. The building is said to be haunted by the ghost of a former keeper, whose footsteps are occasionally heard on the stairway leading to the lantern room.

MICHIGAN

Big Sable
Point

Ludington • Scottville

Lake
Michigan

Pentwater • Crystal Valley

Points, and unwary navigators, steering a course too close to the shore, may run aground on either. To make this less likely, both capes are marked by lighthouses.

In 1867, at Big Sable Point, to the north of Ludington, a 112-ft brick tower was completed. Focused by a third-order Fresnel lens, its beacon gave plenty of warning, which helped mariners to reach the safety of the harbor at Ludington. Having become severely weathered by the harsh lakeside climate, the tower was sheathed in protective iron plates during the 1920s. The tower and other station buildings now serve as attractions of a state park, although its beacon remains in operation, nowadays produced by a modern optic.

LITTLE SABLE POINT LIGHT
Meares, Michigan

Rises from the dunes of a lakeside park

To the south of Ludington, the land presses westward once again, forming Little Sable Point, a dangerous obstacle in the path of any vessel moving along the west-central coast of Michigan. In 1874 Little Sable Point, about 30 miles to the north, was marked by a lighthouse with a red-brick tower, its

lantern room rising 107ft above the lakeside dunes. Equipped with the same third-order Fresnel lens, that has been in use here since the 1870s, the station produces a beacon visible from nearly 20 miles out in Lake Michigan. The light has been automated since the 1950s, but the old keeper's residence was torn down many years ago. The only surviving station building is the tower, which is now a favorite attraction of visitors to Silver Lake State Park.

GRAND HAVEN PIER LIGHTS

Grand Haven, Michigan

Pier lights point the way to a deep-water harbor

Most of Michigan's pier lighthouses mark harbors along the south-western shore of Lake Michigan, well to the south of Ludington and the Sable Points. Perhaps the most famous of these are the St. Joseph Pier Lights, but others such as those at Grand Haven,

south of Muskegon, are nearly as well-known. Placed one behind the other to serve as range lights, the Grand Haven beacons mark the entrance to a fine deep-water harbor near to the mouth of the Grand Haven river.

Located several hundred feet apart, the towers are linked by an elevated walkway, brightly lit at night. Built during the late 1890s, the inner tower is a 51-ft cylinder, made from bolted-on iron plates, while the other consists of a small lantern, perched on top of the station's fog-signal building.

OPPOSITE: The Big Sable Point and Little Sable Point Lights warn shipping of the risk of running aground on these two large capes. Big Sable (left) is iron-clad for protection against the elements, while Little Sable (below right) is of red brick. Both are automated and functional.

BELOW: The Grand Haven Pier Lights are range beacons, like St. Joseph's, designed to help ships reach the safety of the deep-water harbor at the mouth of the Grand Haven river.

LIGHTHOUSES OF AMERICA

HOLLAND HARBOR LIGHT
Holland, Michigan

Big Red is as bright as ever

So striking is the color of the Holland Harbor Lighthouse, that it has long been known to sailors and local admirers as 'Big Red.' Built in 1936, the square, red tower is attached to the keeper's residence, both having been replacements of an earlier structure dating to 1872. During the 1970s, the

FAR LEFT & BELOW: Nicknamed 'Big Red,' the Holland Harbor Light, like many of the lights along the eastern shore of Lake Michigan, is located at the end of a pier. A replacement of an earlier light, the unusual twin-gabled structure was built in 1907. In 1936, the current light tower was added to the top of one of the gables, and the entire building was covered with steel plates.

Coast Guard announced plans to demolish the lighthouse and establish a new, more efficient light on the north side of the entrance channel to Holland Harbor. However, Big Red was so well-loved by the local people that their protests caused the Coast Guard to reconsider. As a result, Big Red's light still shines and is still focused by the station's original sixth-order lens.

SEUL CHOIX POINT LIGHT
Manistique, Michigan

The only safe choice on the north side of Lake Michigan

OPPOSITE & FAR LEFT: During the 17th and 18th centuries, the shores along the north side of Lake Michigan had very few safe harbors, so that when fur-traders discovered one that was suitable, they named it Seul Choix, meaning, the 'only choice.' Its importance was eventually recognized by the authorities and a lighthouse was established there in 1895.

The fur-trading French voyageurs, who frequented the shores of Lake Michigan during the 17th and 18th centuries, were aware that useful harbors on the north side of the lake were in short supply. In fact, safe harbors were so hard to come by that the one near present-day Manistique, on the Upper Peninsula, was given the name Seul Choix, meaning 'only choice.' Eventually, maritime officials would also come to recognize the importance of the harbor and mark it with a major coastal light. Completed in 1895, the station consists of a 78-ft conical brick tower, with a two-story keeper's residence attached. The light

MICHIGAN

BELOW: The Round Island Light was abandoned in 1947, and left to fall into an advanced state of disrepair. Fortunately, it has since been restored, and is now used as a private aid to navigation.

OPPOSITE RIGHT: Mariners used to dread the 80 miles of unlit shoreline that stretched east from Grand Island to Whitefish Point. To fill the gap, Au Sable Point Light was established in 1874, and was a welcome addition to Lake Superior's dark shores.

remains in operation, but the third-order Fresnel lens, that has been in place here for more than a century, has been replaced by a modern aerobeacon.

ROUND ISLAND LIGHT
Mackinac Island, Michigan

Featured in a popular 1980s movie

The red-and-white square lighthouse, that can be seen from the popular resort hotels on Mackinac Island, dates from 1895. In the evening, its light brightens the approaches to the local harbor, but for nearly half a century after the station was retired in 1947, its lantern room remained dark. The abandoned structure had deteriorated almost beyond the point of repair by the 1980s, when the lighthouse was featured in the melodramatic movie, *Somewhere in Time*, featuring Christopher Reeves. The movie generated publicity and won friends for the neglected lighthouse, which has since been restored and returned to service as a private aid to navigation. The light is solar-powered.

MICHIGAN

166

AU SABLE POINT LIGHT
Grand Marais, Michigan

Brightens Superior's dark southern shore

For many years there were few major lights on Lake Superior, and navigators struggled to keep their vessels clear of the lake's dark, unmarked shores. Whitefish Point, near the eastern end of the lake, received a light during the 1860s, but to the west, ship captains were forced to rely on their instincts and good luck. Of course, their luck did not always hold, and the consequences were often tragic. To improve their odds, the Lighthouse Board ordered construction of a number of lighthouses along the southern and western shores of the lake. One of these was completed in 1874, at Au Sable Point, near Grand Marais, on Michigan's Upper Peninsula.

The 87-ft brick tower was built immediately adjacent to the station's rambling two-story keeper's residence. The two were attached by an enclosed walkway, so that the keeper could tend the light without having to brave the blood-freezing temperatures that gripped the lakeshore, before the lakes themselves froze over, and were closed to navigation for the winter. Perhaps due to global warming, the lakes no longer

consistently freeze in winter, but during the 19th and early 20th centuries, this station and most others on the Great Lakes were usually closed from December through to March. The Au Sable Point Light is still in operation, but has been automated since 1958.

MARQUETTE HARBOR LIGHT
Marquette, Michigan

The red lighthouse is as bright during the day as it is at night

Marquette became a key Upper Peninsula port as early as the 1850s, when iron and other valuable ores were discovered in the nearby Michigan and Wisconsin mountains.

The light station here dates to 1853, but the existing square brick tower, and attached two-story keeper's residence, were completed in 1866. An automated modern optic has now replaced the fourth-order Fresnel lens that was in place here for more than a century. Even so, the harbor light can still be seen each and every evening of the year. Painted bright red, the structure itself may be as useful to mariners during the day as its light is at night.

BIG BAY LIGHT
Big Bay, Michigan

Guests get a glimpse of how lighthouse keepers lived

The Coast Guard has now automated lighthouses along every U.S. coast, including those located on the shores of the Great Lakes. Once the keepers were removed and reassigned to other duties, their former dwellings were often allowed to fall into ruin. Many of these large and comfortable homes have now

OPPOSITE: Perched picturesquely on rocks at the entrance to Marquette Harbor, this bright-red lighthouse makes a useful point of reference for daytime mariners. The Marquette Harbor Light was built in 1853, and a keeper's residence was added in 1866.

BELOW: The Big Bay Light is now automated, and its keeper's residence has been converted into a comfortable bed-and-breakfast establishment. Here, visitors are given a taste of what life was once like on a busy light station.

been converted for use as private residences or businesses. The two-story brick residence, at the Big Bay Lighthouse on Lake Superior, has been made into an attractive bed-and-breakfast inn, where overnight guests get a taste of what life would once have been like at this remote station. In place since 1896, the light is still in operation.

EAGLE HARBOR LIGHT
Eagle Harbor, Michigan

A veteran lighthouse that has weathered Superior for more than 130 years

Near to the western end of Michigan's Upper Peninsula, a curving finger of

OPPOSITE: The Big Bay Light at dusk.

ABOVE: The automated light at Big Bay is still in operation.

land points back toward the east. This is the 60-mile Keweenaw Peninsula, and it has been frequented by ore-carrying

freighters for more than 150 years. During the 1850s, the discovery of copper and iron, in mountains to the south and west, caused small ports, such as Eagle Harbor, to become established. To make it easier for ships to get in and out of these ports safely, the federal government built a string of beacons, most of which have long since gone. But the beacon at Eagle Harbor, near the Keweenaw Peninsula's upper end, still lives to tell the tale.

The existing octagonal brick tower, with its attached dwelling, were built in 1871 to replace an earlier lighthouse, that had been overwhelmed by the harsh Lake Superior weather. The station's original fourth-order Fresnel lens has since been replaced by a modern optic.

OPPOSITE & THIS PAGE: During the 1850s, the discovery of copper and iron ore in mountains to the south and west, caused small ports, such as Eagle Harbor, to become established. The red-brick Eagle Harbor Light Station, built in 1851 and replaced in 1871, guards the rocky entrance to Eagle Harbor, guiding mariners across the northern edge of the Keweenaw Peninsula.

Minnesota

*L*ocated near the heart of the North American continent, and more than 1,000 miles from the salty waters of the open Atlantic, Minnesota is nonetheless a mariner's state. The presence of the locks at Sault Ste. Marie and the Saint Lawrence Seaway, means that ocean-going vessels regularly visit Minnesota's primary port facilities at Duluth, to take on loads of wheat, corn, or ore from the state's prodigious iron mines. Today, the wharves at Duluth are not as active as was once the case, but thanks to the productivity of the U.S. steel industry, it has long been one of America's busiest ports. Generations of lake navigators piloted long, narrow freighters to Duluth, then out again with their heavy loads. A few, such as the doomed SS Edmund Fitzgerald, never made it to their destinations, however. The 729ft-long Fitzgerald, steamed out of Duluth on 9 November 1974, ran into a fierce blizzard the following day, and mysteriously sank with all hands into the murky depths of Lake Superior.

The Fitzgerald was neither the first nor the last big freighter to be lost on the lakes. Thousands of vessels of all types have succumbed to storms, ice, or collisions with rocks or shoals on Lake Superior alone. Not one of its 31,820 square miles is entirely safe, but the most dangerous part is certainly its far-western reaches, where it washes against the rocky cliffs of Minnesota. To guide lake freighters, shuttling in and out of port, and help them to keep a safe distance from the shore, the Lighthouse Board established a line of maritime beacons, stretching from Duluth to the Canadian border. Among these are several of America's most historic light stations, one of them being the yellow-brick tower, set atop lofty Split Rock, which is ranked by many as one of the most beautiful lighthouses in the world.

SPLIT ROCK LIGHT
Two Harbors, Minnesota

Some say its the world's most beautiful lighthouse

Although it was decommissioned in 1969, Minnesota's Split Rock beacon remains as bright as ever in the minds of lighthouse enthusiasts and the old-time sailors who had relied on it for so long.

Established in 1910, just as the American steel industry was beginning to flourish, the Split Rock Lighthouse

served as a traffic light of sorts, that governed the flow of ore freighters shuttling back and forth to Duluth. Most of these enormous vessels followed the safer, northerly route through Lake Superior, and this meant passing very near to the stony cliffs, located north-east of Two Harbors. The lighthouse enabled them to find their bearings and keep a safe distance from the deadly rocks along the shore.

Built with yellow brick, Split Rock's octagonal 54-ft tower is not particularly tall, but the great limestone cliff on which it stood placed the focal plane of its beacon more than 170ft above the lake. From this elevation, the bright beacon, focused by the station's third-order Fresnel lens, could be seen from a distance of up to 22 miles. Although the light is no longer in operation, the lens has been left in the tower, which is now part of a popular maritime museum complex.

The station's Fresnel optic is of an unusual type, known as a bivalve lens. Arranged in a slightly rounded disc shape, something like a clamshell, its prisms funnel light into a bull's-eye lens, which further focuses it into an intense beam. When the lens rotates, the light appears to flash.

Located high up on a limestone cliff, the Split Rock Light towers 170ft over Lake Superior. Although no longer in use, it is a popular tourist attraction.

MINNESOTA

TWO HARBORS LIGHT
Two Harbors, Minnesota

Keepers kept warm here when blizzards howled

Overlooking Lake Superior's Agate Bay, Two Harbors Lighthouse may not be as famous or scenic as the Split Rock Light, but it is equally as historic, being the oldest operating lighthouse in Minnesota.

Construction began in the spring of 1891 and the light was placed in service two years later. Two Harbors' bright-red combination tower, moreover, is no less distinctive than Split Rock's yellow tower. The station's 50-ft square tower is attached to the side of the two-story brick dwelling, a feature no doubt once appreciated by its keepers, once blizzards began to sweep over the lake in the late fall. Automated in 1982, the station has no full-time keepers nowadays, and the former dwelling is used as a bed-and-breakfast establishment and museum.

DULUTH SOUTH BREAKWATER LIGHTS
Duluth, Minnesota

A maritime link with Minnesota's mountains of iron

MINNESOTA

Silver Creek

Two Harbors

Arnold

Duluth

Lake Superior

Proctor

WISCONSIN

OPPOSITE LEFT: Established in 1891, the Two Harbors Light is Minnesota's oldest lighthouse. Automated in 1982, the lighthouse is currently a bed-and-breakfast establishment, run by the Lake County Historical Society. The grounds are attractively kept, and visitors are able to climb the lighthouse's square 50-ft tower.

OPPOSITE RIGHT & FAR LEFT: The Duluth South Breakwater Lights mark the breakwater at the head of the Duluth Ship Channel, where it extends out into Lake Superior. The channel is only 300ft wide, and it is always busy as freighters and ore-carriers hasten to make their deliveries before the port freezes over in winter.

At the turn of the 20th century, Duluth became a key shipping point for the ore that was being mined in Minnesota's Mesabi Mountains. To guide the ore freighters to the city's loading facilities, the government established a number of modest pier and breakwater lights near to the entrance of the harbor. Among these were the Duluth South Breakwater Lights and the Duluth Pier Lights, the latter operating from a pair of towers on a long, concrete harbor pier. Located at a distance from one another, the two lights functioned as range beacons, marking the safest, most direct channel into the harbor. All three Duluth towers still stand, and their lights are still in operation.

The South Breakwater Lights were built in 1901, the inner light being located beneath the drawbridge. Its steel-frame tower is 67ft tall, and it has a fourth-order Fresnel lens. The outer light still has its green fourth-order Fresnel lens.

MISSISSIPPI

*A*lthough Mississippi has less than 50 miles of coastline, about the same as neighboring Alabama, it has had more than its fair share of lighthouses. As many as a dozen official government stations once marked, not only the state's stormy Gulf of Mexico coast, but also the meandering bayous of the Mississippi Delta. Unfortunately, having fallen victim to war, wind, water, and time itself, nearly all of Mississippi's historic lighthouses have vanished. But for Mississippians, the names of these fallen towers – Ship Island, Cat Island, Horn Island, Round Island, Merrill's Shell Bank, Lake Borgne, East Pascagoula, Pass Christian, and others – still have the power to evoke memories of a long maritime heritage, while also recalling incidents in a violent past.

The original Ship Island Lighthouse was built in 1853, partly as a result of Congressional lobbying on the part of Jefferson Davis, then a Mississippian senator. But after Davis became president of the Confederate States during the Civil War, his Ship Island Light was captured and utilized by Union forces, intent on blockading the Mississippi coast. The original lighthouse was so badly damaged during the war, that it was eventually demolished and replaced by a pyramid-shaped wooden tower, clad in weatherboarding. Probably intended as a temporary structure, the seemingly flimsy building proved surprisingly sturdy, serving for almost a century before finally succumbing to a fire, accidentally started by tourists in 1972.

Mississippi's Horn Island Lighthouse proved far less durable, however. Built on a low bank of silt, near the mouth of the Pascagoula river in 1874, it was under threat of erosion almost from the start. During its first 30 years of service, the lighthouse, having been buffeted by continual storms, was either pulled apart and reassembled on higher ground, or even rebuilt, at least half a dozen times, before it was finally obliterated by a hurricane in 1906. The storm, perhaps equal in destructive force to the recent cataclysmic Katrina, tragically carried away Horn Island's keeper, Charles Johnson, along with his wife and children.

There was one Mississippi lighthouse that some regarded as indestructible: this was the one, built in 1859, on Round Island near Pascagoula. Its stout brick tower survived not only the Civil War, but also numerous hurricanes, including the one that destroyed the Horn Island Light. It even withstood the ravages of time and neglect after it was abandoned by the Coast Guard in 1946. Then, in 1998, Hurricane Georges arrived, which although not an unusually destructive storm, having done only moderate damage to nearby Pascagoula, was nevertheless able to deliver a mortal blow to the Round Island Light. A preservation society in Pascagoula is raising funds to rebuild the fallen tower.

BILOXI LIGHT
Biloxi, Mississippi

Its iron shell has made it all but impervious to hurricanes

The gracious city of Biloxi lies directly on the Mississippi Sound, separated from the Gulf of Mexico by a string of barrier islands. Here, a grand old veteran of the Civil War still stands, having survived not only America's great fratricidal conflict, but also the punishment dealt it by countless storms. In 1968, the Biloxi Lighthouse was able to withstand Hurricane Camille, which all but destroyed the city itself, and more recently Hurricane Katrina, which swept these coasts in 2005 with a violence that few could have imagined. The iron shell,

that encases the Biloxi Light's brick-and-mortar tower, is no doubt the reason for its survival.

Built in 1848, the white 61-ft tower has stood on the Biloxi waterfront, within sight of Beauvoir, the historic home of President Jefferson Davis, who led the Confederacy during the Civil War. For many years following the war, the tower was painted black, some say as a sign of mourning following the assassination of President Abraham Lincoln, Davis's nemesis.

The Biloxi Lighthouse is also notable in that several of its keepers were women: Mary Reynolds, one of the nation's first female lighthouse keepers, tended the light throughout the Civil War, before finally retiring in 1866. Later female keepers also included Maria Younghans who, with her daughter Miranda, maintained the light for more than 62 years from 1867 to 1929.

OPPOSITE PAGE & LEFT: Built in 1848, the Biloxi Light was possibly the first cast-metal lighthouse to appear in the south. The light was operated by civilians from 1848 to 1939, and is notable for having several female lightkeepers, including Maria Younghans, who with her daughter tended the light for a total of 62 years. In 1939, the U.S. Coast Guard assumed responsibility for the light's operation, and after being declared surplus to requirements in 1968, the Biloxi Light passed into the hands of the city of Biloxi.

NEW HAMPSHIRE

*N*ew Hampshire has exceptionally strong commercial, cultural, and historic links with the sea, considering it has only 13 miles of coastline. Settled by fishermen during the early 1600s, New Hampshire was at first regarded as part of Massachusetts, but in 1679 became a separate colony. Located on the banks of the Piscataqua river, Portsmouth served as the colony's main port, becoming a major center of shipbuilding and a hub of maritime trade.

To mark the approaches to Portsmouth Harbor, a light was established near the Piscataqua river entrance during the early 1770s. At first, this humble aid to navigation consisted of nothing more than a simple oil lantern, hung from a tall pole, located in the grounds of a stone fortress at the mouth of the river. A soldier, stationed at the fort, would have received extra pay to light the lantern each night, before hoisting it with a pulley to the top of the pole. Before long, however, it was replaced by a wooden tower with a lantern room at the top.

The fort and its lighthouse were destined to play an important role in the American Revolution. In 1774, with a British fleet blockading Boston Harbor, Portsmouth citizens raided the fort and confiscated its stock of gunpowder. It is said that the keeper of the Portsmouth Light, John Cochrane, helped to drive a wagonload of the precious powder to patriot forces, who had dug in on Breed's Hill, outside Boston, where a crucial battle was fought on 17 June 1775.

A number of notables have visited Portsmouth over the years, including the Marquis de Lafayette, although his opinion of the lighthouse is not known. A French aristocratic, Lafayette volunteered to lead American troops during the Revolutionary War. He appeared in Portsmouth in 1882, just as the war was drawing to a close. Nearly a decade afterwards, by which time lighthouses had become the concern of the fledgling federal government, President George Washington himself paid the lighthouse a visit. He was far from pleased with its condition, however, and being the keeper's virtual employer, Washington had him fired.

fortress guns were fired, their vibrations shattered windows, upended lamps, and broke optical equipment inside the lighthouse. The shaking eventually cracked the walls of the building, allowing rain and rot to penetrate.

A more sturdily-constructed lighthouse was completed in 1804, and its 80-ft octagonal wooden tower stood until 1877. The tower seen here today is of a type pioneered in the mid-19th century, and consists of a 48-ft iron cylinder, constructed of bolted-on iron plates. All but impervious to the effects of rain, wind, and high water, this structure would have remained unfazed by cannon blasts. Indeed, it has stood the test of time, and is still an active aid to navigation after more than 150 years of hard service. Focused by a fourth-order Fresnel lens, its fixed green light can be seen from a distance of about 12 miles.

OPPOSITE: The Portsmouth Harbor Light has evolved from humble beginnings during colonial times to the tower seen here today. Dating from the mid 19th century, the present lighthouse has stood the test of time, and is still an active aid to navigation after more than 150 years of service.

PORTSMOUTH HARBOR LIGHT
Portsmouth, New Hampshire

A patriotic light stands guard at Fort Constitution

The lighthouse guiding vessels into the Piscataqua river today bears little resemblance to the one that marked Portsmouth Harbor during colonial times. The crude pole-and-lantern beacon, that served Portsmouth during the early 1770s, was replaced by a wooden tower with a lantern room, shortly before the beginning of the Revolutionary War. The lighthouse was located in the vicinity of Fort Constitution – then known as Fort William and Mary. When the big

NEW JERSEY

*D*uring the first few years of the colonial period, what is now known as New Jersey was part of New York. The two colonies went their separate ways shortly after the English seized them from the Dutch in 1676, but there has always been some confusion as to where the state of New York ends and New Jersey begins. There are some who say that Staten Island should be in New Jersey, since it is closer to Elizabeth, Newark, and Jersey City, and considerably more than a short bridge-crossing or ferry-ride from downtown Manhattan. The territorial disputes between the two states have even extended to ownership of a lighthouse.

In 1764 an octagonal stone light tower was built near the end of an extensive sand spit, not far from the seaside community of Highlands, New Jersey. Interestingly, however, the lighthouse was neither built nor owned by citizens of New Jersey, but had been erected by New York City businessmen, to mark the entrance to the Lower New York Bay, and point the way to their wharves on Manhattan Island. During the Revolution, Continental forces tried but failed to destroy the tower to keep it from falling into British hands, and it became the focus of a very different sort of conflict following the war, which took the form of a legal tug-of-war between the newly independent states of New Jersey and New York. Despite the fact that New Yorkers had built the tower, and had maintained its light for years, New Jersey laid claim to what was then known as the New York Lighthouse. Eventually, New Jersey was forced to hand the facility over to the new federal government in 1789.

In return for handing Sandy Hook over to the government, New Jersey would receive plenty of new lighthouses over the years – all of them built with Congressional funding. As many as a dozen major lighthouses would be established to guide ships along the state's long, beautiful, and often quite dangerous coastline. These included the twin towers at Navesink, where the U.S. conducted its earliest experiments with Fresnel lenses, the giant brick Barnegat tower, and the exquisite white cylinder at Cape May, all of them now famous and among the best-loved structures in America.

SANDY HOOK LIGHT
Highlands, New Jersey

New Jersey's oldest lighthouse once belonged to New York

Although not the oldest light station in America, Sandy Hook does have the oldest original maritime tower. While the lights at Boston (established in 1716), Brant Point, Massachusetts (1746), and New London, Connecticut (1760), came earlier, and while all three beacons still guide mariners, their

Since the first explorers charted the coastline of what is now New Jersey, the hills in the vicinity of Lower New York Bay have served as a sort of natural beacon, warning mariners away from a dangerous landfall and guiding them into the Hudson river. But the hills are of little use to navigators in the dark, so in 1828 the government established a beacon there to assist mariners at night. For some reason, federal maritime officials decided to give the lighthouse a fortress-like appearance, and a pair of towers, located at either end of a long, parapeted stone wall, made it possible for the station to display a pair of lights – known as the Twin Lights of Navesink.

In 1841, Navesink became the first light station in America to utilize a Fresnel lens. It would also be the first, in 1883, to use kerosene as a lamp fuel and in 1898 to use electric lamps. For many years, a first-order Fresnel lens brightened the south tower, while the lantern room of the north tower held a revolving second-order lens. In 1952, the south tower was deactivated, and its enormous lens is now on display in the Navesink Twin Lights Museum, near the lighthouse. The north tower still displays a light, but now uses a sixth-order lens.

original towers were long ago destroyed and rebuilt. The tower at Sandy Hook is the same octagonal rubblestone tower that was built in 1764, and it looks very much today as it did more than 240 years ago.

Sandy Hook's third-order Fresnel lens is an extraordinary piece of equipment that has functioned continuously for more than 150 years and focused the station's beacon on more than 50,000 nights. Remarkably, it is no less effective today than when it was installed in 1857, several years before Abraham Lincoln was elected to the U.S. presidency. Its light still guides vessels into the Lower New York Bay and it can be seen from points along the southern shore of Staten Island, also from Long Island, and from New Jersey's northern shore.

NAVESINK LIGHT
Highlands, New Jersey

The first lighthouse in America to use a Fresnel lens

NEW JERSEY

SEA GIRT LIGHT
Sea Girt, New Jersey

The retired lighthouse is back in business

With its two-story Victorian house, its square tower rising just above its roofline, the Sea Girt Lighthouse looks more like a typical New Jersey seaside home than a hard-working navigational station. However, the black, cast-iron lantern room, at the top of the tower, reveals the building's true purpose – that of guiding vessels along the New Jersey coast. Built in 1896, the ruddy-brick lighthouse handled this task efficiently for more than half a century before the Coast Guard decided to deactivate its light in 1955.

Like more than a few other decommissioned lighthouses, it was destined to have a second career. After decades of use as a community center for the tiny Borough of Sea Girt, the building was refurbished and its light restored during the 1980s. The building now does double duty as a museum and as a private aid to navigation.

BARNEGAT LIGHT
Long Beach Island, New Jersey

Old Barney was designed by a Civil War general

Those who know and love this historic maritime tower, refer to it fondly as 'Old Barney.' The red-and-white mammoth brick structure, seen here today, dates from 1857, when it replaced an earlier and much smaller lighthouse that had been knocked down in a storm. Rising more than 170ft above the Atlantic waves, the big tower was in part the work of George Meade, the innovative engineer who designed and built lighthouses during the years preceding the Civil War.

When he became a Union general, Meade's battle plans seemed to be no less robust than his structures, and his design for Barnegat proved especially sound; despite more than 150 years of bombardment by Atlantic gales, the tower's thick walls still stand tall. More damaging than storms, perhaps, were the decades of neglect that followed the decommissioning of the Barnegat Light in 1944. Although left to deteriorate to a state of near ruin, the structure was not fatally wounded, and a $660,000 restoration program returned it to a pristine condition in 1991. A nearby museum houses the station's original first-order Fresnel lens.

HEREFORD INLET LIGHT
North Wildwood, New Jersey

Clones of this lighthouse are in California

Smaller lighthouses, built during the mid-to-late 19th century, were often made of wood. For the sake of efficiency, the tower was either attached to, or was made part of, the primary station residence. Sometimes several such lighthouses were built using a single, basic set of blueprints. In 1874, the Lighthouse Board ordered work to commence on a pair of California

NEW JERSEY

lighthouses, both consisting of a wooden, stick-style Victorian residence wrapped around a square tower. That same year, a lighthouse of very similar design was completed on Hereford Inlet, near North Wildwood, New Jersey, having most likely been built using the same set of plans. Consequently, Hereford Inlet Light, Point Fermin Light, near Los Angeles, and the East Brother Light, near San Francisco, are near clones of one another.

Although it was built for only $25,000, the Hereford Inlet residence, and integral 50-ft tower, have stood the test of time. It even survived the ferocious hurricane that devastated the New Jersey coast in 1889, when it provided a refuge for local residents, whose homes had been washed away. After the station was closed by the Coast Guard in 1964, the building fell into disrepair; it has since been restored, however, and its light has been returned to active service.

CAPE MAY LIGHT
Cape May, New Jersey

Where New Jersey dips its toe into the Atlantic

At the far southern end of New Jersey, a toe of land extends nearly 20 miles into the Atlantic. This prominent peninsula helps to define Delaware Bay, and also presents a formidable navigational hazard to seamen, entering or exiting the bay. So that navigators could more correctly judge the entrance, and remain at a safe distance from the shore, the Lighthouse Board ordered the construction of a tall light tower at Cape May. Completed in 1859, the 157-ft brick tower has guided mariners for more than 150 years, its powerful light visible for up to 25 miles out at sea.

The longevity of the massive tower is most likely due to its double-walled construction, the brick structure being essentially a tower within a tower. Although the light remains active, the lighthouse itself is leased to and maintained by Cape May's Mid-Atlantic Center for the Arts.

SHIP JOHN SHOAL

Fortesque, New Jersey

A Victorian oddity in Delaware Bay

Surely one of the strangest-looking structures to be seen anywhere, the Ship John Shoal Lighthouse is an odd combination of fussy Victorian architecture and solid cast-iron construction. Positioned directly over a dangerous shoal, near the middle of Delaware Bay, the lighthouse sits on a massive cylindrical iron caisson, partially sunk into the subsurface mud. This secure foundation has allowed the station to survive more than 125 years of sea storms and constant use.

In contrast to the huge caisson beneath, the tower is a rather fanciful structure, with a high-pitched mansard roof. Although rather bizarre, considering the tower's open-water location, its style reflects the prevailing tastes of the 1870s, when the lighthouse was built. The Ship John Shoal beacon continues to warn ships, but its original fourth-order Fresnel lens has now given way to a solar-powered modern optic.

FAR LEFT: This is the third lighthouse to have been built on Cape May Point. The first was built in 1823 and had a tower 68ft tall, while the second, that was 78ft tall, was built in 1847. Both are now underwater, due to the erosion of the shoreline.

BELOW: The Ship John Shoal, and the lighthouse that marks the spot, got their name from an incident that happenened there in 1797. The cargo ship John *was returning from Germany to Philadelphia, when it fell foul of a shoal near the mouth of the Cohansey Creek. The passengers and crew made it safely to the shore, but the vessel unfortunately sank and was broken up by the ice floes.*

NEW YORK

*A*s nearly everyone knows, New York is the business and maritime heart of America, and this has pertained since the earliest days of colonization. Henry Hudson recognized the strategic and potential commercial importance of the Lower and Upper New York Bays, when he explored them in 1609, giving his name to the river from which they were formed. Later, the Hudson river, and the excellent anchorages it offered, attracted Dutch settlers, the inflections of whose language can be detected in the clipped tones of New Yorkers today. The English took over the colony in 1664 and, like the Dutch before them, recognized the importance of New York's coastal position. British forces clung tenaciously to the port through much of the Revolutionary War, eventually surrendering it to the newly independent United States.

New York's continuing prosperity is as much due to its sea trade as it is to the efficient transportation provided by the Great Lakes. It is the only state with two distinct coasts – three, if the shorelines of Lakes Ontario and Erie are considered separately. Yet these advantages would have made far less impact on the history of New York, and that of the nation, had it not been for the navigational lights that directed ships to New York City, Albany, Rochester, Buffalo and other key ports.

In 1764, New Yorkers built one of the first lighthouses in America at Sandy Hook, which was actually located in New Jersey rather than New York, and was to be the subject of a dispute. In time, other maritime beacons would mark the shores of Long Island, the Hudson, and Lakes Ontario and Erie. Many of these lights remain in service today and some, such as the Montauk Point Light, established in 1797, have been in continuous operation for two centuries or more – longer than the Statue of Liberty has watched over New York Harbor. There are some New Yorkers who consider the lighthouses to be no less a monument to New York's spirit and heritage than the lady herself.

MONTAUK POINT LIGHT
Montauk, New York

President Washington's liberty light

It is said that, before the Revolutionary War, George Washington visited Montauk Point at the far-eastern end of Long Island, and that he considered it an excellent site for a future maritime beacon. Years later, when he became president, Washington made his vision a reality by ordering construction of a lighthouse atop the sandy Montauk bluffs. Completed in 1797, shortly after Washington had left office and retired to his farm in Virginia, the Montauk Point Lighthouse was among the finest and tallest buildings erected during the 18th century. The 78-ft sandstone tower, with its handsome two-story keeper's dwelling, was indeed impressive, and it should have been, since the cost to the government was in excess of $22,000, the equivalent of a respectable family fortune at that time.

There were those who considered the lighthouse far too expensive, but these same critics, were they alive today, would have realized that no grounds for

complaint exist. The lighthouse still stands, and its light has remained in service for over 210 years, at a cost to the federal treasury of less than 30 cents a day.

During the station's early years, a variety of oil lamps and reflectors produced its beacon, but later the light was focused by a large Fresnel lens. Today the light is generated by a modern aerobeacon.

For many immigrants fleeing from Europe, a glimpse of the Montauk Point on the horizon would have been the first indication that their refuge was near.

OPPOSITE RIGHT BELOW: The Montauk Light's current beacon is equivalent to 2,500,000 candle power.

THIS PAGE: The Montauk Light was completed in 1797 on the specific instructions of President George Washington. The Montauk Historical Society now owns and maintains the lighthouse.

FIRE ISLAND LIGHT
Off West Islip, New York

A coastal skyscraper issues a warning to mariners

The lighthouse originally built on Fire Island, in 1827, was never very effective. At 74ft, its tower was too short and its oil lamps too dim to produce a beacon visible from more than a few miles out at sea. All too often, navigators would steer their vessels into the natural minefield of shoals, south of the island, having caught not so much as a glimpse of the light. Sometimes this had tragic consequences, as in 1850, when the freighter *Elizabeth* plowed into the shoals and sank with heavy loss of life and property. As it turned out, the tragedy helped to focus the attention of Congress on the inadequacies of the entire U.S. lighthouse system. By 1852, Congress had created a Lighthouse Board, appointing as advisors only the best-qualified engineers, scientists, and military officials.

During the 1850s, the board upgraded many existing light stations and launched a wide-ranging construction program. Among the many new towers built during the 1850s was the 168-ft brick giant on Fire Island. Completed in 1858, and equipped with a top-quality Fresnel lens, it had both the height and the optical technology to warn vessels while they were still far out in the Atlantic. In fact, the powerful first-order lens could focus a beacon visible from a distance of up to 25 miles.

Eventually, improvements in navigational technology and offshore beacons would render even this first-rate facility obsolete, causing the Coast Guard to decommission the light and abandon the old tower in 1974. The deteriorating structure might well have been demolished as a public hazard, had not a determined local preservation organization come to the fore. Handsomely restored and relit, Fire Island's veteran tower has now been returned to service as a tourist attraction and a private aid to navigation.

TIBBETS POINT LIGHT
Cape Vincent, New York

Guardian of the gate to the Great Lakes

More than 750-miles-long, and essentially a liquid highway, the Great Lakes have contributed mightily to the prosperity of the nation as a whole and of New York in particular. Ocean-going freighters are able to penetrate as far inland as Chicago or Duluth, near to the very heart of the continent, by following

OPPOSITE: The Fire Island Light originally stood only 200 yards from the western edge of the island, but miles of beach have been added to the island during the past century or more.

LEFT & PAGES 192–193: Tibbets Point Light marks the point where Lake Ontario flows into the St. Lawrence river, a few miles west of the village of Cape Vincent.

PAGE 192 LEFT: The first Fort Niagara Light was established in 1782, atop the 'French Castle', a structure still located within Old Fort Niagara. The current beacon was deactivated in 1993, having been replaced by a light beacon at the U.S. Coast Guard Station, Niagara.

the St. Lawrence Seaway as it winds its way through the lakes. Vessels enter or exit the lakes by way of the St. Lawrence river, and nearly all that do so pass within sight of Cape Vincent's Tibbets Point Lighthouse.

This strategically located light station, at the eastern end of Lake Ontario, was established in 1827. However, the existing 68-ft brick-and-stucco tower dates to 1854, when it replaced an earlier stone structure. The fourth-order Fresnel lens, installed in the lantern room at that time, still focuses the Tibbets Point beacon. The station lost its keeper, however, though not its light, when the beacon was automated in 1981. Some consider it to be the most beautiful scenic lighthouse on the eastern Great Lakes.

FORT NIAGARA LIGHT
Youngstown, New York

Points the way to Niagara Falls

The first official navigational light on the Great Lakes was established by the British, rather than the Americans. During the Revolutionary War, the British ordered the construction of a stone tower to guide freighters bound for the strategic Niagara Portage, at the eastern end of Lake Ontario, whence

men and supplies proceeded overland, skirting the Niagara Falls to arrive at the shores of Lake Erie. From there they could be transferred by ship to distant settlements and outposts located on the upper lakes.

After the war, the tower and its beacon were dismantled, but a new light was established near the site of the original in 1823. It stood atop the walls of Fort Niagara, which had played an important role in three major conflicts: the French and Indian War, the Revolutionary War, and the War of 1812. At first, the new lighthouse assisted freighter traffic feeding the portage, but within a few years, the opening of the Erie and Welland Canals had rendered it more or less obsolete. It continued, however, to serve as a harbor beacon for Fort Niagara and the minor port of Youngstown.

The existing Fort Niagara Lighthouse dates to 1872, when a 50-ft stone tower was built beside Lake Ontario, a little to the south of the old fort. Its height was increased to 61ft in 1890, and the tower still stands. Having guided lake traffic for more than a century, its beacon was finally deactivated in 1993. Today, the lighthouse is an attraction of Fort Niagara State Park.

CHARLOTTE-GENESEE LIGHT
Rochester, New York

A school campaign saved the Great Lakes' oldest tower

The first U.S. lighthouse on the Great Lakes was completed in 1822, near to the mouth of the Genesee river at

SODUS POINT LIGHT
Sodus, New York

A stone lighthouse now serving as a museum

Another early Great Lakes beacon once shone from Sodus Point, near the entrance to Sodus Bay, an attractive anchorage on Lake Ontario. Here, in 1825, the government built a rough stone tower, not unlike the one completed three years earlier at the mouth of the Genessee river, two dozen or so miles to the west. But the Sodus

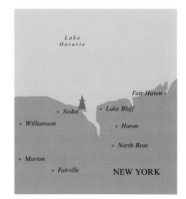

Rochester, New York. Shining from atop a 40-ft octagonal tower, built of rough stone, it guided freighters in and out of the city's harbor and along the shores of Lake Ontario. Over the years, sand and silt, deposited by the river, steadily pushed the shoreline further from the tower, making its light less effective for navigation. Finally, in 1884, the government removed the tower's lens and established a more useful light closer to the lake.

The tower stood empty and abandoned for more than 80 years – for longer, in fact, than it had served as an active lighthouse. By the 1960s, its crumbling walls were thought to be a hazard, and the Coast Guard announced plans to demolish the historic structure. A campaign of letter-writing by students at a local high school raised awareness of the tower's plight, and the government, in the face of public protest, decided to spare the old building. In 1984, a full century after its light was extinguished, the tower's beacon was restored. Today, it is focused by a fourth-order Fresnel lens, similar to that used during the 19th century. Once more an active aid to navigation, the tower also serves as the key attraction of a local history museum.

RIGHT: The Thirty Mile Point Light was so named because it is 30 miles east of the mouth of the Niagara river, which empties into Lake Ontario.

OPPOSITE PAGE & PAGE 198: The Point Gratiot Light, built in Victorian Gothic style. In 1984, the grounds of the lighthouse were leased by the Coast Guard to the Chatauqua County Armed Forces Memorial Park Corporation, a non-profit-making organization. The lighthouse is now the Dunkirk Lighthouse Museum.

THIRTY MILE POINT LIGHT

Somerset, New York

One of America's first electric lighthouses

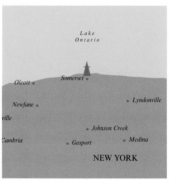

Built in 1876, the Thirty Mile Point Lighthouse was similar in construction to the one at Sodus Point, completed a few years earlier. The 61-ft limestone tower was attached to the station residence, enabling keepers to attend to their duties in winter, without having to brave blizzards and subzero temperatures. Its light focused by a third-order Fresnel lens, the station guided vessels along the Lake Ontario shore to the east of Niagara. In 1885, Thirty Mile Point became one of the first maritime beacons in America to be powered by electric lamps. The experiment proved highly successful, and soon afterwards the new-fangled light bulbs began to be installed in lighthouses everywhere.

The lamps were extinguished and the lighthouse was deactivated in 1959, after more than 80 years of service. Now owned by the state, the lighthouse serves as a popular attraction of New York's Golden Hill State Park. In 1998, its light was recommissioned as a private aid to navigation.

Point Light had obviously not been as well constructed as the long-lasting Charlotte-Genessee tower, since, by the end of the Civil War, it had become beyond repair.

A new Sodus Point Lighthouse was built to take its place in 1871. Its 45-ft square stone tower was attached to the station residence, so that it would be easier for the keeper to tend the light during the winter months. The lighthouse was decommissioned and replaced by a nearby pierhead beacon in 1901. Today, the historic building is the home of an informative and attractive maritime museum.

.

POINT GRATIOT LIGHT
Dunkirk, New York

Whale oil proved more reliable than gas

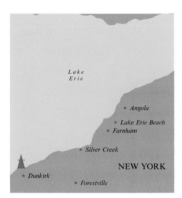

Whereas the experiment with electric lamps succeeded at Thirty Mile Point, a similar 19th-century attempt to use natural gas lighting at the Point Gratiot Lighthouse, in Dunkirk, was doomed to fail. Several attempts were made to fuel the station's lamps with gas, pumped

from nearby wells, but performance was never satisfactory.

The beacon, established in 1826, was powered primarily by whale oil until the station was converted to electricity during the 1890s. Regardless of the light source, the beacon has been focused by the same third-order Fresnel lens since 1857, which is powerful enough to project a fixed light signal, visible from 16 miles out on Lake Erie. Nowadays, the Point Gratiot Lighthouse serves not only as an active aid to navigation, but also as a museum and military memorial.

SELKIRK LIGHT
Pulaski, New York

The lantern burns once more after 130 years in the dark

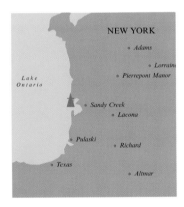

Established in 1838, the Selkirk Light shone for little more than 20 years before being taken out of service during the 1850s. Over the years, the two-story, fieldstone lighthouse was used as a small hotel and for a variety of other purposes. Then, remarkably, in 1989, the old station was restored to life, when its light was re-established as a private aid to navigation. Nowadays the historic lighthouse is also used as overnight accommodation, mostly by sportsmen, who visit the area hoping to sample the excellent fishing in the area. The octagonal tower stands on the roof of the original keeper's residence, supporting an unusual bird-cage lantern – a style not widely used since before the Civil War.

Sitting at the mouth of the Salmon river, the Selkirk Light dates from 1838, having been in service for little more than 20 years.

North Carolina

A bewildering maze of shoals, shallows, inlets and
sounds, the waters off the complex coast of North
Carolina have claimed thousands upon thousands of
ships and the lives of countless mariners, which is why
it is often referred to as the 'Graveyard of the
Atlantic.' Especially hazardous are the Outer Banks,
the chain of narrow barrier islands that extend for
about 130 miles, and that separate North Carolina's
brackish coastal estuaries from the open sea. For
hundreds of years, large and small vessels have been
caught in the grip of the Outer Banks, where they have
been torn to shreds by the waves.

Recognizing the grave threat these islands
posed to shipping, the federal government made an
attempt to mark the Outer Banks as early as 1803.
North Carolina's first lighthouse was designed by
Henry Dearborn, a hero of the Revolutionary War,
who served as Secretary of War in the administration
of Thomas Jefferson. Dearborn's lighthouse at Cape
Hatteras, however, did not fare so well in its war with
the Atlantic, neither did any of the other early
lighthouses located up and down the Outer Banks. Its
height limited by the technology of the time, the Cape
Hatteras tower of 1803 was the loftiest at 95ft, but the
others were not sufficiently tall to serve as effective
coastal beacons. Even worse, their outmoded lamp-
and-reflector optics were not bright enough to warn
ships away from the extensive shoals lurking by the Outer Banks, some of which extended many miles out
into the Atlantic. More than one sea captain complained of his ship running aground, while he frantically
searched for a guiding light.

This unfortunate state of affairs would change for the better during the 1850s, after the Lighthouse
Board took charge of U.S. maritime lights. Highly negative reports concerning the condition of the lights
along the Outer Banks (the Cape Hatteras beacon was described as 'the worst light in the world') spurred
Lighthouse Board engineers into launching a vigorous construction program, which some historians have
likened, in boldness and relative scale, to the U.S. space program during the 1960s. Within only a few years,
the Outer Banks would be protected by a wall of soaring maritime sentinels, fitted with powerful Fresnel
lenses that were the most advanced and expensive equipment available at the time.

Built between 1858 and 1870, North Carolina's great coastal towers at Cape Hatteras, Bodie Island,
Currituck Beach, Cape Lookout, and elsewhere, have survived wars, hurricanes, and the shifting sands of
time. Several are still equipped with the same dazzling crystal lenses that have focused their beacons for a
century and a half. Besides being of vital importance to mariners, they are possibly even more important
nowadays as symbols of North America's rich maritime heritage.

CAPE HATTERAS LIGHT
Cape Hatteras, North Carolina

*America's most famous and best-loved
lighthouse*

Soaring nearly 200ft above the dunes,
near the tiny Outer Banks community of
Buxton, the Cape Hatteras Lighthouse is
the second of two lights to have warned
captains against steering their ships too
close to the cape and its deadly shoals.
At 95ft tall, the first lighthouse was one
of the tallest structures of its day, but its
beacon was still not high enough to be
seen by vessels, before they ran aground
in the extensive shallows.

One of the most dangerous maritime
obstacles in the world, the spreading
Outer Banks shallows, were created by
the interaction of the cold Labrador
Current with the highly dynamic warm-
water Gulf Stream. These two great
oceanic phenomena slam into one
another, just off the Outer Banks,
creating fog and foul weather, and piling
up the sands left behind by the last ice
age. To better assist seamen navigating
these turbulent waters, the Lighthouse
Board hired contractors to add 50ft of
brick to the original Cape Hatteras
tower. The enlarged structure was then

equipped with an especially powerful first-order Fresnel lens. After the Civil War, however, an entirely new tower was built, and thanks to a near miracle of preservation, it still stands today.

The sands of the Outer Banks are always on the move, and for more than a century after the lighthouse was completed in 1870, erosion threatened to undermine the mighty Cape Hatteras tower. The ocean advanced almost to the

LEFT: The Cape Hatteras Light, seen from its original position on the beach. It was moved to a safer location about 1,600ft inland, due to the erosion of the shoreline.

BELOW: The Cape Hattaras Light, after it had been moved to its new, safer location.

BELOW: The Bodie Island Light is as popular with visitors as the Cape Hattaras Light, 40 miles or so to the south. This, the present lighthouse, was completed in 1872 with the help of a government grant. It was designed by architect Dexter Stetson, who also designed the current Cape Hatteras Lighthouse.

OPPOSITE RIGHT: The Carrituck Beach Light was built to fill the 'dark spot,' that existed between the light at Cape Henry, Virginia and that at Bodie Island. Like other lighthouses on North Carolina's Outer Banks, the Carrituck Beach Light still serves as an aid to navigation.

edge of the tower's foundations on more than one occasion, only for it to recede once more as natural processes rebuilt the beach. As the end of the 20th century approached, however, it seemed that the relentless Atlantic would finally claim its victim. Waves now almost engulfed the tower, and it seemed that it would surely topple over during the very next storm.

Fortunately, the Cape Hatteras Lighthouse had friends in both government and private circles. During the late 1990s, an extraordinary, expensive, and ultimately successful, effort was made to save the historic tower. In a notable feat of engineering, the 3,500-ton brick structure was lifted

onto rails and moved, a few inches at a time, to a new, less vulnerable position more than a quarter of a mile from the rapidly-eroding beach.

Today, the spiral-striped tower receives a steady stream of visitors at its new home, approximately 1,600ft from the ocean; those arriving at nightfall can see the beacon illuminating the skies over the Outer Banks, just as it has for nearly 150 years. The station lost its huge first-order lens long ago, and the light is now produced by a rotating aerobeacon, similar to the type used in airports. Badly damaged by vandalism, the original Cape Hatteras lens, or what is left of it, can be seen at the nearby Outer Banks Maritime Museum.

BODIE ISLAND LIGHT
Nags Head, North Carolina

Helping mariners to avoid the ocean's graveyard

Built by a contractor with insufficient experience, and with a far too stringent budget, the Bodie Island Lighthouse, completed in 1848, proved to be of little use to mariners. Intended to assist navigators, after they had possibly lost sight of Cape Hatteras's beacon, about 40 miles to the south, the Bodie Island tower and its light were inferior in almost every way. Built on marshy foundations, and unsupported by piles, the tower began to sink even before its

Nowadays, the Bodie Island Lighthouse serves not only as a life-saving beacon, but also as a popular attraction of the Cape Hatteras National Seashore, where the station's two-story keeper's residence is used as a visitor center and museum. Visitors, for reasons of safety, are prohibited from climbing the tower, but at night, its enormous first-order Fresnel lens can be seen and enjoyed from the ground, flooding the lantern room and the surrounding countryside with light. The beacon can be seen from about 20 miles out in the Atlantic.

CURRITUCK BEACH LIGHT
Corolla, North Carolina

A red-brick tower crowned with a shining crystal lens

Having completed the 193-ft Cape Hatteras tower in 1870, and the 163-ft Bodie Island tower only two years later, Lighthouse Board construction crews moved on to the tiny town of Corolla, located near the north end of the Outer Banks. Here they erected the 158-ft brick tower of the Currituck Beach Lighthouse, which was commissioned for service in 1875.

last brick had been laid. The station's lamp-and-reflector optic proved so ineffective, that captains often ran their vessels aground without even having noticed the light at all.

During the late 1850s, the leaning tower was demolished and replaced by a much sturdier structure, which would serve for less than two years before Civil War raiders extinguished its lamps. Confederate troops stacked gunpowder in the tower, before blowing it up, to prevent it from falling into Union hands.

After the war, the Lighthouse Board undertook the daunting task of restoring the lighthouse and the many others that had been damaged or destroyed during the conflict. Bodie Island Light was rebuilt by some of the same masons and laborers responsible for building the existing Cape Hatteras tower, and having completed that lighthouse in 1870, they moved on to Bodie Island, completing its new 163-ft brick tower by the fall of 1872. Unlike the original, the foundations of the new tower were of solid granite, firmly anchored to the island by means of iron piles. So sound were its structural underpinnings, that the tower has survived hundreds of gales and hurricanes and stands as straight today as it did when recommissioned more than 130 years ago.

Like the other colossal lighthouses on the Outer Banks, this was intended to warn ships away from the shoals and shallows that spread eastward from the islands, its powerful beacon allowing navigators sufficient time to change direction and follow a new course.

Still focused by the same first-order Fresnel lens, that was installed more than 130 years ago, the Currituck Beach beacon can be seen for up to 20 miles, but visitors willing to climb the station's winding staircase can see it from close quarters. The old light station now serves as a tourist attraction and museum as well as a coastal seamark.

Most light towers are painted with bold and distinctive patterns to help mariners recognize them during the day. Cape Hatteras's tower, for example, sports black-and-white spirals, while that of Bodie Island is painted with broad black-and-white bands. Currituck Beach tower, however has been left unpainted, leaving its red bricks as its sole distinguishing feature.

CAPE LOOKOUT LIGHT
Cape Lookout, North Carolina

A survivor of the Civil War continues to guard Horrible Headland

Marking the south-western extremity of the Outer Banks is the oldest of North Carolina's lofty maritime towers. The lighthouse located on Cape Lookout today, was completed around the same time as the second of Bodie Island's lighthouses, in 1859. But unlike the tower at Bodie Island, about 100 miles to the north, Cape Lookout's mammoth 156-ft tower survived the Civil War; the unmistakable black-and-white diamond pattern of its tower is still a familiar sight to mariners, entering Onslow Bay and heading for

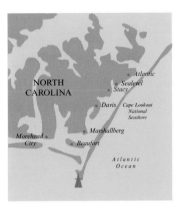

anchorages near Beaufort, Morehead City, and Wilmington.

The existing Cape Lookout Lighthouse was not the first to be built. An earlier structure, completed in 1812, once stood here for more than a generation before it was replaced shortly before the Civil War. The original tower was of an unusual design, having brick walls sheathed in a protective cocoon of wood. The structure itself functioned well, but as with other early maritime lights along the Outer Banks, its beacon did not. The light was weak and ineffective, and it could not be relied upon to warn mariners of the shoals, lying off what came to be known as 'Horrible Headland.'

The construction of the new tower in 1859, rendered Cape Lookout much less horrible for mariners, and the shipwrecks that had once occurred with sickening regularity suddenly became rare. Much of the improvement was due to the station's huge first-order Fresnel lens, which focused the beacon for more than a century before it was removed shortly after the light was automated in 1967. Nowadays, an aerobeacon produces the station's flashing light, which is visible from an impressive distance of up to 25 miles.

FAR LEFT: The Cape Lookout Light is at the lower end of a string of islands, referred to as the Outer Banks of North Carolina. There are four other lighthouses on the Outer Banks: the Currituck Beach Light, the Bodie Island Light, Cape Hatteras, and the Ocracoke Island Light. All but Ocracoke are coastal lights.

ABOVE & OPPOSITE LEFT: The Ocracoke Island Light. Ocracoke Inlet was first put on the map when English explorers wrecked a sailing ship there in 1585.

OPPOSITE RIGHT: The Bald Head Light was the 18th lighthouse to be established in America and the third built by the federal government. It was built to mark the Bald Head Shoals, Jay Bird Shoals, and Frying Pan Shoals. It also guides shipping entering the Cape Fear river, bound for the port of Wilmington.

OCRACOKE ISLAND LIGHT

Ocracoke Island, North Carolina

Marks the former hideout of Blackbeard the pirate

Ocracoke's first lighthouse was built in 1803, making it a contemporary of the original Cape Hatteras tower. It stood on Shell Island, not far from the former hideout of Blackbeard, a notorious 18th-century pirate. In 1718, however, near Shell Island, a colonial expeditionary force was able to corner

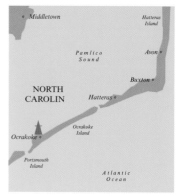

and kill Blackbeard, along with most of his gang.

By the early 19th century, the greatest danger confronting mariners in these waters was not pirates, but hurricanes and shipwrecks. When skies grew leaden and winds began to howl, as they so often did in the fall, the modest Ocracoke Island Light offered a welcome refuge from the storm.

The first Ocracoke Island tower stood for only about ten years before it was struck and felled by a bolt of lightning. A second tower was completed in 1818, this time on the

LIGHTHOUSES OF AMERICA

BALD HEAD (CAPE FEAR) LIGHT
Bald Head Island, North Carolina

North Carolina's first lighthouse

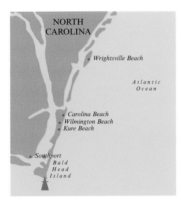

Established on Bald Head Island, during George Washington's last full year as president in 1796, the lighthouse was built to mark the entrance to the Cape Fear river. In 1813, beach erosion destroyed the tower, but it was rebuilt in 1817, performing its task effectively until well into the 20th century.

In 1935, however, the venerable structure was retired and its light extinguished. Although its lantern has been dark now for generations, the old lighthouse remains standing and serves today as an historic monument and museum – a reminder of the early days of the U.S. Lighthouse Service.

The 100-ft Bald Head tower is octagonal, with massive walls around 7ft thick at the base. The interior of the tower is not open, as is the case with most other lighthouses, but divided into levels with rooms where the keeper lived and worked. The very top level once held the station's whale-oil lamps and reflectors.

banks of the inlet linking the small town of Ocracoke with Pamlico Sound. This 65-ft cone-shaped structure still stands, its light guiding ferries and other vessels to Ocracoke Island. Having served mariners more or less continuously for 180 years, the Ocracoke Island Lighthouse is North Carolina's oldest operational station. Automated in 1955, it displays a fixed white light that can be seen from a distance of up to 14 miles.

OHIO

*T*he considerable prosperity of this quintessential Midwestern state would never have been possible without the commerce generated by the Great Lakes. Ohio's iron furnaces were fed with ore brought from Minnesota and Michigan in long lake freighters, and in this way an endless variety of manufactured goods and agricultural products were shipped to markets in other states. Cleveland and Toledo can still be included among the Great Lakes' busiest ports, and the vessels approaching them, along Ohio's extensive Lake Erie shoreline, are still guided by maritime lights, some of them established nearly two centuries ago.

Built in 1821, the Marblehead Lighthouse, near Sandusky, is the oldest active light station on the lakes, while the Fairport Harbor Light has been shining since 1825. These, and a number of other Ohio maritime beacons, can still be seen from the waters of Lake Erie, and occasionally still save lives, especially when the lake is torn by summer gales or winter blizzards. But the historic towers, producing these guiding lights, now serve an additional, educational purpose, emphasizing the importance of maritime commerce in the history of Ohio and the Midwest.

station's beacon continues to shine out over Lake Erie, just as it has on approximately 65,000 previous occasions.

Although there have been few changes elsewhere, the means of producing the beacon has continued to evolve. Originally, the light was generated by oil lamps, enhanced by reflectors, but after 1858, the beacon was focused by a high-quality fourth-order Fresnel lens. Nowadays, however, a modern plastic optic is used to produce the light signal, which flashes every six seconds; the green light can be

FAR RIGHT: The Marblehead Light is the oldest continuously operating lighthouse on the Great Lakes. It was originally called the Sandusky Bay Light, because it marked the entrance to Sandusky Bay and the eastern end of the south passage between the Bass Islands and the Ohio shore. Its name was changed to the Marblehead Light in 1870.

MARBLEHEAD LIGHT
Bay Point, Ohio

Still shining after 190 years

One of the oldest aids to navigation to have been in continuous operation in North America is the Marblehead Light. The inscription 1821, marking the doorway of the conical limestone tower, is not an address but the year in which the structure was completed, and surprisingly little has changed in the almost 190 years since. Each night, the

seen from a distance of about 11 miles.

Located near Port Clinton, a few miles north-west of Sandusky, the venerable lighthouse is maintained by the Ottawa County Historical Society, while the keeper's dwelling is now used as a museum.

FAIRPORT HARBOR LIGHT
Fairport, Ohio

Links the Erie Canal with the American heartland

The opening of the Erie Canal, during the early 1820s, linked the waters of Lake Erie in the west to the Hudson river in the east, unleashing a tide of immigration and commerce that turned sleepy lakeside communities into bustling ports. One of these was the small town of Fairport, where a key beacon was established in 1825. The commercial freighters and passenger vessels, having negotiated the canal from points east, often stopped here for supplies and fuel, and the Fairport Harbor Light guided them into port.

The Fairport Harbor Light. The original beacon not only guided vessels, but also served as one of the northern terminals of the 'Underground Railroad' – a loose network that provided aid and assistance to fugitive slaves during the Civil War.

OHIO

VERMILION LIGHT
Vermilion, Ohio

A midget replica lights the way to one of America's finest maritime museums

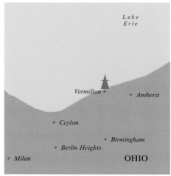

ABOVE: *Interior of the Fairport Harbor Light.*

FAR RIGHT: *The Vermilion Light, although a replica, is historically correct. It stands proudly in front of the Great Lakes Historical Society, on the shores of Lake Erie.*

For nearly half a century, a small 30-ft tower supported the station's lantern room and optic, but by the late 1860s, the harsh lakeside weather had taken its toll of the structure. In 1871 it was replaced by a 69-ft sandstone tower, fitted with a third-order Fresnel lens. The new lighthouse remained in operation until 1925, when it was decommissioned. Today, the tower, and the adjacent two-story keeper's residence, serve as the home of a fine maritime museum.

The red-and-white octagonal tower, standing near to Vermilion on the shores of Lake Erie, is only 16ft tall. It stands on a bank, however, adding about 20ft to the elevation of its fixed, red light. The beacon serves as a private aid to navigation, while the tower provides the popular Inland Seas Maritime Museum with its attractive display.

The tower standing at Vermilion today is not the original, although it is an historically accurate replica. The original tower, built in 1877, was removed in 1929 and was replaced with a nearby pier light.

OREGON

*B*etween the Columbia river and the California border, for a distance of 300 miles, the green hills and mountains of Oregon cascade into the blue Pacific Ocean. Created by volcanoes and the titanic thrusts of opposing continental plates, the Oregon coast is being ceaselessly etched and carved by waves and tides, creating a natural work of art that is forever in progress. Oregonians refer to this spectacular meeting of land and water as the 'Emerald Coast,' which may, if anything, be to understate its great beauty.

This holds little appeal to mariners, however, as they struggle to safeguard their vessels. The reason for this is simple: the coastal mountains, that provide so much of Oregon's scenic wonder, do not stop at the water's edge, but continue westward far out into the ocean, their peaks rising from the sea floor to a point just below the surface. No right-minded mariner would intentionally venture into this deadly minefield, and those that have blundered unintentionally into these waters, or have been driven here by storms, have almost invariably perished.

Since the first settlers arrived in Oregon from the east, in wagons rather than in ships, ways have been sought to attract more shipping and maritime commerce to the area. This has been neither an easy nor an altogether successful task; during the latter half of the 19th century, Oregon was given a considerable boost, when a chain of lighthouses, marking its coast from Astoria in the north, and stretching all the way to the California border, were constructed. Perched on cliffs or set along the banks of wild and lonely rivers, they rank among the loveliest in North America.

HECETA HEAD LIGHT
Near Florence, Oregon

Picture-perfect for postcards

Although by no means the oldest of Oregon's maritime beacons, the Heceta Head Lighthouse may possibly be the most beautiful. Its setting is so impressive that motorists, driving along U.S. Highway 101, are invariably compelled to stop and stare in wonderment, feeling they must record what they seeing in a photograph or two. Some may even be able to stay here for a while, should there be a vacancy, because the keeper's residence is now a bed-and-breakfast inn.

As with most of the Oregon coast, the same geological forces that made Heceta Head beautiful also made it hazardous for mariners. An undersea mountain range extends well out to the west, its peaks lurking just beneath the

surface of the waves, waiting to rip the hull of any ship that strays. To help seamen maintain a safe distance, the government established a light station here in 1894.

The 56-ft masonry tower, with its two-story keeper's dwelling, proved anything but easy or inexpensive to build. Materials had to be brought in by ship and put ashore at a landing stage on the nearby Suislaw river. They were then loaded onto wagons and pulled along steep mountain tracks to the construction site. It took two years to

OPPOSITE BELOW & THIS PAGE: Constructed in 1874, the Heceta Head Light was named for the Spanish explorer, Don Bruno de Heceta. Its beacon, visible for more than 20 miles out at sea, is the most powerful on the Oregon coast.

complete the project, which ended up costing the federal treasury no less than $180,000, a sum considered quite astonishing at that time.

The imported first-order Fresnel lens, placed here in 1894, remains in use. It has 640 individual crystal prisms, each of which have been painstakingly polished by hand. Like many other Fresnel lenses, this produces a flashing light when rotated. Originally, the lens was turned by clockwork machinery, driven by weighted cables, but nowadays, of course, electric motors perform the task. Although Heceta Head's tower is not particularly tall, it stands on a cliff that allows its beacon to range out over the Pacific from an elevation of more than 200ft, making its light visible from a distance of more than 20 miles.

YAQUINA BAY LIGHT
Newport, Oregon

Built in the wrong place because someone could not read a map

Built in 1871, the two-story wooden dwelling and red tower, located on the north side of Yaquina Bay, is one of the oldest standing lighthouses in the west. Strangely enough, however, although it was perfectly sound, and its lamps were in good working order, it has not been in commission for more than 130 years, and was in active use for less than three. It is said that the reason for its short life was that someone – most likely a government bureaucrat – misread a map. In 1874, a tall cylindrical light tower was mistakenly constructed on Yaquina Head, when it should have been built on Cape Foulweather, 15 miles to the north. It was decided to keep the new lighthouse, however, rendering the Yaquina Bay beacon obsolete. Yaquina Bay was eventually converted for use as a life-saving station, and now serves as a museum.

YAQUINA HEAD LIGHT
Newport, Oregon

Helps when shipboard compasses start to spin

There should never have been a lighthouse on Yaquina Head. The 93-ft brick tower was completed in 1874 and is a classic example of the towers of the period. It was supposed to have been built on Cape Foulweather, some 15 miles to the north, but according to legend contractors began to build it on Yaquina Head instead, and by the time anyone noticed the mistake, a handsome tower had been built and was being made ready for service. Rather than demolish it, however, it was decided to close the existing Yaquina Bay Lighthouse, and use the new facility at Yaquina Head instead.

The first-order lens, placed here more than 130 years ago, still focuses the powerful Yaquina Head light signal, which can be seen from more than 20 miles away. The beacon helps mariners to avoid becoming confused and falling prey to a local geological anomaly. Here, a heavy concentration of magnetized iron in the rocks causes shipboard

compasses to malfunction, making navigators more likely to steer their vessels dangerously off-course.

UMPQUA RIVER LIGHT
Winchester Bay, Oregon

An Oregon frontier beacon

During the 1850s, a major lighthouse construction program, aimed at marking the nation's western coast, was launched by the federal government. Most of the first 20 or so western towers were

OPPOSITE LEFT & ABOVE : The Yaquina Bay Light is one of the west coast's oldest lighthouses. It was made obsolete when the Yaquina Head Light came into being, and is now a museum.

OREGON

station was placed at a safer distance from the flood-prone Umpqua's steadily eroding banks. Located on a bluff, about 100ft above the river and the Pacific, the new station was given a 60-ft brick and stucco tower, while a first-order Fresnel lens provided the beacon with the power it needed to reach vessels 20 miles or more out in the Pacific. The flashing red-and-white Umpqua River Light has been automated since 1966, but it is still focused by the original lens. Nearby, a delightful museum occupies the former Coast Guard station.

CAPE ARAGO LIGHT
Coos Bay, Oregon

Guiding lumber freighters since 1866

The combination tower and keeper's residence, located on Cape Arago in 1934, was the last lighthouse to be built

located in California or Washington, but Oregon, still regarded as something of a frontier region, was not altogether ignored. In 1857, a key light station was established near the mouth of the Umpqua river, not far from Reedsport, a bustling lumber-milling and shipping center. Unfortunately, the original station was destroyed by erosion in 1864, and would not be replaced for nearly 30 years.

In 1894, another attempt was made to mark the river mouth. This time, the

in Oregon and one of the last to be built anywhere in the United States. Its beacon marks the entrance of the commercially vital Coos river, and points the way to the thriving port of Coos Bay. During the mid 19th century, Coos Bay mills processed vast quantities of lumber, which were shipped to

216

markets in San Francisco, San Diego, and Asia, in freighters loaded at docks along the Coos river.

A lighthouse with an octagonal iron tower was first placed on Cape Arago in 1866, to guide these vessels safely in and out of port. When the original tower became threatened by erosion, however, it was replaced by a wooden lighthouse in 1909.

The existing structure dates from 1934. The station's classic fourth-order Fresnel lens, used in one or other Cape Arago tower since 1866, was eventually removed and replaced by a modern, solar-powered optic, allowing the light to be seen from a distance of about 16 miles. The station was automated in 1966 but decommissioned in 2006.

COQUILLE RIVER LIGHT
Bandon, Oregon

Beloved by surfers, campers, and romantics

For many years, the Coquille River Lighthouse looked like one of the shipwrecks it was designed to prevent. Built in 1895, it was abandoned soon after the Coast Guard took charge of the Lighthouse Service in 1939. After this, it was neglected for decades, with the result that it was all but destroyed by wind, rain, and vandals. Eventually, the sadly-deteriorated building became a part of Bullards Beach State Park, and

rather than demolish the structure, state officials decided to restore it instead. Today, the lighthouse's unusual Victorian Italianate architecture can be admired from the waterfront streets of Bandon, which are lined with busy shops and restaurants.

OPPOSITE PAGE: The Umpqua River Light.

LEFT: The Cape Arago Light.

BELOW: The Coquille River Light.

PENNSYLVANIA

*T*hose unfamiliar with the history and geography of Pennsylvania may imagine it to be a landlocked inland state, with little in the way of a maritime heritage. Nothing could be further from the truth: Pennsylvania was founded by William Penn, the Quaker son of a prominent British sea admiral, and as was the case with the other colonies, most early Pennsylvania immigrants, some of whom were themselves seamen, arrived by way of a long Atlantic sea crossing. Philadelphia, the colony's principal city, had a direct link with the Atlantic Ocean, via the Delaware river and bay, making it a thriving seaport, which it is to this day, while in the west, Pennsylvania had a very different, but nonetheless important maritime link, in that it had access to the Great Lakes.

It may have been an accident of history, but Pennsylvania was destined to play an important role in one of the most decisive naval battles of all time. During the War of 1812, the protected harbor at Presque Isle, known today as the port of Erie, Pennsylvania, was a key U.S. naval base. A small fleet of hastily constructed warships set sail from Erie during the late summer of 1813 to confront the British fleet, which until that point dominated the Great Lakes. The turning point of the war came with Oliver Hazard Perry's victory over the British fleet in the Battle of Lake Erie, 10 September 1813, which made it possible, in the following month, for General Harrison to invade Canada and defeat the British and Indians in the Battle of the Thames River. Shortly after the battle, Perry sent ashore his now famous message: 'We have met the enemy and he is ours, two ships, two brigs, one schooner, and one sloop.'

Another, less direct, result was that Erie became and remains to this day an active port city on the Great Lakes. It is also the home of Pennsylvania's only official lighthouse: its tower marks the end of a long, sandy peninsula, that stretches its protective arm around the small bay that serves as Erie's primary harbor. The peninsula and light station both bear the name Presque Isle, meaning 'almost an island,' in French.

PRESQUE ISLE LIGHT
Erie, Pennsylvania

An historic light marks the Friendship State's principal harbor

After the Revolutionary War, having no access of its own to the Great Lakes, Pennsylvania purchased the pointed, western tip of New York state, and in this way acquired 45 miles of frontage on Lake Erie. This new territory included a harbor of notable importance at Presque Isle, which would come to be known as Erie, Pennsylvania.

The first lighthouse at Erie was built in 1819, on a hill overlooking the harbor. Although active until 1890, it was inadequate, in that it was too far from the lake to be able to guide vessels approaching the harbor entrance. In time, this task would be assigned to a beacon, shining from the tip of the peninsula sheltering the harbor.

Completed in 1873, and still in operation, the Presque Isle Lighthouse (right) consists of a 68-ft square brick tower attached to a two-story keeper's residence. Although once focused by a fourth-order Fresnel lens, the station's beacon is now produced by a modern optic. The dwelling now serves as the residence of a manager of Presque Isle State Park.

RHODE ISLAND

*C*overing only 1,045 square miles, Rhode Island, in terms of land area at least, is by far the smallest state in the Union. But in spirit, however, it is much, much larger. As Rhode Islanders see it, the ocean and all of its bounty belongs to them, and this has been their attitude since the colony of Rhode Island came into being during the 1600s. The colony began as a collection of plantations, huddled against the shores of an enormous estuary, known as Narragansett Bay. It would eventually become a prosperous state, with several sizeable manufacturing centers and numerous cities, towns, and villages – all with their faces toward the sea.

The infamous pirate, Captain William Kidd, used Narragansett Bay as a hideout during the 1600s, and he is reputed to have buried some of his ill-gotten gold and other booty in the sandy soil of Conanicut Island, near the entrance to the bay. Years after Captain Kidd was captured by the British and hanged for his crimes, a different sort of gold began to brighten the shores of Conanicut Island. It was the glow of the Beavertail Light, which first shone forth in 1749. Although set fire to by the British during the Revolutionary War, the Beavertail Lighthouse was eventually rebuilt, and it has now served mariners for more than 250 years. Although not as old as the veteran Beavertail sentinel, half-a-dozen other lighthouses have also guided Rhode Island mariners, for the better part of two centuries, some of which are among the finest still-operational light towers in America.

BEAVERTAIL LIGHT
Jamestown, Rhode Island

America's third oldest lighthouse was once set fire to by the British

When the Beavertail Light was established on Conanicut Island, near the entrance to Narragansett Bay in 1749, there were only two other lighthouses in the whole of what is now the United States. Those earlier sentinels

were the Boston Lighthouse, established in 1716, and Nantucket's Brant Point Light, established in 1746. The Beavertail Light was different from its predecessors in that it faced out onto Rhode Island Sound, rather than onto the open sea; but it was just as necessary, since the storms that lashed the sound could be quite as violent as the ones out in the Atlantic Ocean.

The first Beavertail tower, a simple wooden structure, was burned down by British troops as they retreated from Rhode Island during the Revolutionary War. Following the war, a sturdier tower was built, which was in service until 1856, when the existing 45-ft granite tower and two-story, brick keeper's residence were completed. Although automated in 1972, the lighthouse remains active, and its flashing white signal continues to guide mariners. Nowadays, the keeper's residence houses a fascinating maritime museum.

ROSE ISLAND LIGHT
Newport, Rhode Island

Saved from destruction and restored by local preservationists

Ships guided by the Beavertail Light into Narragansett Bay, soon encounter narrows and shoals. To help seamen navigate them, the Lighthouse Board ordered construction of a light station on Rose Island, near the middle of the channel. Built atop an abandoned stone fort, an octagonal wooden tower, with a residence for its keeper, was completed in 1870. The Rose Island Lighthouse served mariners for almost exactly a century before its beacon was rendered obsolete by the nearby Newport Bridge, completed in 1969.

Dwarfed by the soaring bridge, the little lighthouse was closed in 1971, following which, wind, rain, and

OPPOSITE BELOW CENTER & LEFT: The Beavertail Light, completed in 1856, replaced an earlier wooden structure built in 1749. The southernmost part of Conanicut Island is known as the Beavertail, because of its shape. This rocky, windswept point looks south toward Rhode Island Sound and beyond to the Atlantic Ocean, and separates the east and west passages of Narragansett Bay.

PAGES 222–223: The attractive little Rose Island Light became obsolete when the massive Newport Bridge was built in 1969. However, the heavily vandalized lighthouse was rescued and restored, and is now used as a private aid to navigation.

PAGE 223 RIGHT: The Newport Harbor Light was automated in 1963 and continues to emit a fixed green light, illuminated by a 250-mm modern optic.

RHODE ISLAND

Middletown

Jamestown

Fort Adams State Park

Newport

Atlantic Ocean

vandalism caused so much damage to the historic structure that the Coast Guard decided to demolish it. Thanks to the efforts of local preservationists, however, the building was saved. The Rose Island beacon has been rekindled and now functions as a private aid to navigation, while the building, having been attractively refurbished, is used as a museum and lodging for guests, wishing to sign themselves up as 'keeper of the week.'

NEWPORT HARBOR LIGHT
Newport, Rhode Island

A light that welcomes the rich and famous

North of the Beavertail Light, and across from Rose Island, is Newport Harbor, an historic anchorage that attracts an incongruous mix of commercial fishing boats and fabulous yachts. During the 19th century, the seaside town of Newport became the summer capital of high society, both American and European, and the aura of affluence was even more pronounced when the international yacht race, known as the America's Cup, took place. This was held at Newport every three or four years, having continued for more than half a century, but even now, when the regatta is held at various locations

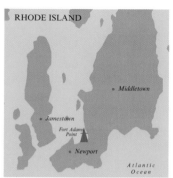

RHODE ISLAND

Middletown

Jamestown
Fort Adams
Point

Newport

Atlantic
Ocean

around the world, Newport continues to attract the rich and famous.

The welcoming green beacon, that guides the yachts and fishing boats into the harbor, was established in 1824. The station's official name is the Newport Harbor Light, but locals refer to it as the Goat Island Lighthouse.

Built on Goat Island, the original tower was relocated after the existing octagonal granite structure was completed in 1842. Its dwelling was damaged in a bizarre accident in 1921, when it was struck by a U.S. Navy submarine, that had veered off-course in heavy fog. It was demolished soon after, never to be replaced. Today, the old tower stands in the vicinity of a grand hotel.

CASTLE HILL AND LIME ROCK LIGHTS
Newport, Rhode Island

Lime Rock was home to 'America's most famous woman'

Castle Hill Lighthouse marks the eastern passage to Narragansett Bay, where its stubby, 34-ft conical granite tower has been a key local seamark for more than a century, having changed very little since it was built in 1890. Its black cast-iron lantern displays a red

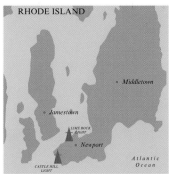

light. The keeper's house is at Castle Hill Cove, some way from the light itself.

The old Lime Rock Lighthouse, located near the heart of the Newport waterfront, is no longer active and is today the home of the Ida Lewis Yacht Club. Its name is no accident, since the

indomitable keeper of the Lime Rock light was, for many decades, a woman of that name, once described as the 'most famous woman in America.' Ida Lewis earned her reputation by single-handedly rescuing a dozen or more drowning victims from the icy waters of

RHODE ISLAND

Newport Harbor. Her fame was heightened by an 1869 article, written about her in *Harper's Weekly* magazine, and by a personal visit from President Ulysses S. Grant. Lewis served as keeper until she died in 1911. It is said that following her death, boats in Newport Harbor continued to toll their bells throughout the night.

POINT JUDITH LIGHT
Point Judith, Rhode Island

Once housed an early flashing light

Few have guarded a greater volume of maritime shipping than Rhode Island's Point Judith Lighthouse. Each year, for the better part of two centuries, this coastal sentinel has made silent contact with thousands of freighters (and been

OPPOSITE LEFT: The Castle Hill Light, that marks Narragansett Bay's east passage, was designed by the prominent American architect, Henry Hobson Richardson, who used his own 'Richardsonian Romanesque' style to harmonize the lighthouse with the Victorian-style mansions nearby.

ABOVE: The Point Judith Light, as it exists today, was established in 1857 and is significant for having utilized one of America's first flashing beacons. It has been referred to as the 'Cape Hatteras of New England,' in that the treacherous waters and rocks surrounding the light have been responsible for numerous shipwrecks.

RHODE ISLAND

A watchtower and a simple beacon were first established at Watch Hill by the Rhode Island colonial government in around 1745, giving the area its name. It may also have been used as an earlier lookout point by Narragansett Indians.

noted in their logs), headed in and out of Long Island Sound and Narragansett Bay. In 1907 alone, the station's keeper probably sighted more than 20,000 passing vessels.

The original lighthouse, built here in 1810, lasted only until 1815, when it was destroyed in a great storm. Replaced with a sturdier structure in 1816, it was rebuilt again in 1857. The new 51-ft brownstone tower proved much stronger than its predecessors and still marks Point Judith after more than 150 years.

The Point Judith Light is significant in that it utilized one of America's first flashing beacons. To make the light flash, early 19th-century engineers placed the optic on a rotating base, turned continually by a giant clockwork mechanism. Even to this day, the station has an odd sort of flashing beacon; the light is on for five seconds, then repeatedly off and on for two seconds at a time, before the cycle begins again. This unusual characteristic has its uses, in that

it helps passing mariners to distinguish Point Judith's beacon from other nearby lights.

WATCH HILL LIGHT
Watch Hill, Rhode Island

Built near the site of an 18th-century military watchtower

To the west of Point Judith, near the Connecticut border, the Watch Hill Lighthouse guards an historic village and a broad stretch of Block Island Sound. The village of Watch Hill got its name from a watchtower, built during King George's War (French and Indian War) in the 1740s. The watchtower fell into ruins over the years and no similar structure marked the spot until 1807, when the first Watch Hill Lighthouse was completed. A round wooden tower, it was equipped with whale-oil lamps and probably served as little more than a harbor light for local fishermen.

By the 1850s, the Lighthouse Board had reached the conclusion that a more substantial lighthouse was needed, to help ships navigate the increasingly crowded sound. Completed in 1857, it consisted of a square 51-ft granite tower, with an attached residence for the keeper. The station has served mariners well for more than 150 years.

Unfortunately, it could not prevent the disastrous loss of the steamer, *Larchmont*, in the waters off Watch Hill in 1907. The steamer collided with an old schooner, during a February blizzard, and both vessels sank with a loss of more than 150 lives.

BLOCK ISLAND SOUTHEAST LIGHT
Block Island, Rhode Island

Loaded onto rollers, it was pushed away from the cliffs

The Gothic-style Block Island Southeast Lighthouse could be described as possibly the most distinctive structure in America. Its red-brick octagonal tower, and attached keeper's residence, bear more of a resemblance to a Victorian mansion than a lighthouse. Nonetheless, a lighthouse it is, and its beacon has probably saved thousands of lives. During the 20 years before the lighthouse was built in 1875, more than 50 schooners and other large vessels ran aground and were wrecked on Block Island's seaward, south-eastern shores, most of them occurring in the vicinity of a line of towering cliffs. The lighthouse was built atop the cliffs and was fitted with an especially powerful first-order Fresnel lens to warn ships away.

After serving mariners for more than a century, the Block Island Light was forced to face its own destruction by the same, rapidly-eroding cliffs. The cliffs were beginning to disappear into the ocean, making it certain that the lighthouse would eventually go the same way.

Fortunately, for those who love old lighthouses and their architecture, a team of innovative engineers found a way to rescue the building. The massive

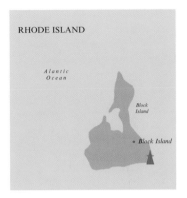

RHODE ISLAND

Atlantic Ocean

Block Island

• Block Island

2,000-ton structure was jacked up onto rollers, and was pushed back, inch-by-inch, until it was a safe distance from the cliff edge. The effort cost almost $2 million, but saved one of America's most remarkable buildings.

LEFT & BELOW: Block Island Southeast Light is a Victorian Gothic-style building, built on the Mohegan Bluff in 1875. It is surrounded by dangerous shoals and ledges, and was sometimes referred to as the 'stumbling block' of the New England coast.

PAGE 228 FAR RIGHT: The Morris Island Light is a reminder of a grand era in American maritime history. What now remains, however, is an old, weathered sentinel, resting precariously on a tiny plot of eroded shoal in the waters off Folly Beach.

PAGE 229 RIGHT: The Hunting Island Light was built of interchangeable cast-iron sections, so that it could be dismantled and moved.

SOUTH CAROLINA

SOUTH CAROLINA

*B*ecause of its strategic estuarine anchorages, South Carolina was the site of early attempts at colonization by the Spanish, French and English, but the English settlement of Charles Town, founded in 1670, was the only one to take root. The new colony maintained a vibrant trading relationship with the mother country, making the village that would eventually become the city of Charleston into a bustling port. As early as 1673, pitch fires were lit to guide supply ships and trading vessels into the harbor, and while this primitive makeshift did make navigation possible, along a coastline crowded with threatening shoals, it did not make it altogether safe.

In 1767 Charleston followed the example of Boston, a generation earlier, by placing a light atop a tall brick tower near to the harbor entrance. The Charleston Lighthouse was one of the first in colonial America, and would serve the city for nearly a century. An octagonal brick tower, soaring more than 100ft above the harbor, it ranked for many years among the tallest structures in North America. Like so many other southern lighthouses, this handsome and historic building was destroyed during the Civil War, the first shots of which were fired within sight of its lantern room. Rebuilt after the war, it is known today as the Morris Island Light, and once again it is poised at the edge of destruction. The threat this time is not from cannonballs or gunpowder charges, but rather from the effects of time and rampaging erosion. Efforts are being made to save the old lighthouse, but it remains to be seen whether or not they will succeed.

MORRIS ISLAND LIGHT
Charleston, South Carolina

A survivor of earthquakes now awash with the tides

When the first Charleston Lighthouse was built in 1767, only a few scattered coastal beacons functioned along the coastlines of North America. Of sturdy construction, the 102-ft octagonal brick structure was the tallest and most impressive of the colonial coastal towers. For more than a century, the Charleston Lighthouse guided naval vessels and trading ships, some of them loaded with African slaves. The tower survived the Revolutionary War, the War of 1812, and countless gales, only to be blown up by Confederate troops during the Civil War.

By 1876, a replacement for the fallen Charleston tower had been completed. A massive cylinder of brick, rising 161ft above Folly Beach, near the harbor entrance, it was painted with black-and-white bands and fitted with a first-order Fresnel lens. Engineers realized the structure would be exposed to fierce storm-force winds and flooding tides, so they built it on a concrete foundation, stabilized by piles driven nearly 50ft into the underlying bedrock. These unusually sound underpinnings enabled the

228

lighthouse to survive the earthquake, that flattened much of Charleston in 1885. The tower has also survived more than a century of tidal erosion.

With nearly the whole of Morris Island eaten away by the hungry tides, the Coast Guard decommissioned the lighthouse in 1962. To mark the harbor, the government then built a truly modern structure, on nearby Sullivans Island, complete with trapezoidal aluminum walls, an elevator, and air conditioning. Left to slowly deteriorate, the abandoned tower on Morris Island has resisted time and erosion longer than anyone thought possible. Today, it is the object of a vigorous preservation effort that may yet save it for future generations.

HUNTING ISLAND LIGHT
Hunting Island, South Carolina

An earlier tower mysteriously vanished from view

The Hunting Island Light was completed in 1859, just as the nation was falling into the chaos of the Civil War. Having functioned for less than two years, the light was extinguished, most likely by Confederate troops, to prevent it from being used to guide Union invasion forces ashore. As it turned out, the nearby port of Beaufort remained in Confederate hands for most of the war, but by the time the fighting ceased in 1865, the lighthouse had vanished. A likely explanation is that it was undermined by erosion and collapsed into the sea.

A second Hunting Island Lighthouse was ready for service by 1875. With the fate of the original tower in mind, engineers gave the station a cast-iron tower, that could be pulled apart and relocated whenever erosion threatened. This would soon prove useful: in 1885, with the crumbling shoreline creeping ever nearer the tower's foundations, the 136-ft structure was dismantled and reassembled about a mile inland.

But its removal, even to this seemingly safe distance, could not protect the tower forever. Over the last century, the shoreline has edged steadily closer, threatening to undermine the tower's foundations once again. Although endangered, the lighthouse remains in service both as an aid to navigation and as an attraction of Hunting Island State Park.

TEXAS

TEXAS

*T*he lighthouses of Texas are closely bound to the extraordinary history of this enormous state. No lighthouses were built here during the centuries that Texas was ruled by Spain or Mexico, nor were there any during the brief period from 1836 to 1845, when Texas was regarded as an independent republic. Some inlets and river entrances may have been lit by signal fires, but the first true lighthouses were built only after the United States had annexed Texas and won the resulting war with Mexico. Consequently, the state's oldest lighthouses date from the mid 19th century

Since they were built after the Lighthouse Board had taken charge of the U.S. system of maritime lights and buoys, the tall towers marking the long arc of coast, from the Louisiana border to Mexico, are mostly well-engineered and well-constructed. Some are made of cast-iron plates, bolted together to form sturdy shells, an innovation that has enabled them to survive numerous hurricanes.

The deadliest hurricane in U.S. history was not the recent Katrina, but rather the 1900 Galveston Hurricane, which took thousands of human lives. The Bolivar Point Lighthouse was one of the few structures to survive the great flood that swept Galveston during the storm, and dozens of refugees escaped certain death by climbing the steps of its tower.

BOLIVAR POINT LIGHT
Galveston, Texas

The first tower was melted down to make cannonballs

Having declared its independence in 1838, Texas became the 28th state of the Union in 1845, precipitating a war with

Mexico that lasted until 1848. After Mexican capitulation ended the conflict, federal maritime authorities launched an effort to mark the 360 miles of desolate beaches and barrier islands that Texas had added to the U.S. coastline. As one of Texas's most important ports, Galveston received special attention, and a cast-iron tower had been erected on Bolivar Point by 1852. Located beside the key inlet of Bolivar Roads, the station marked the city's harbor as well as the entrance to Galveston Bay and the primary shipping channel leading to Houston. However, the station's 65-ft cast-iron tower would stand for only about ten years. During the Civil War it was demolished by the Confederates, its iron plates melted down for weapons.

The 117-ft black tower, seen at Bolivar Point today, was completed in 1872. It consists of a brick cylinder, sheathed in iron to protect it from the often-harsh Gulf climate. This protective suit of armor has been so effective that the tower has withstood countless gales and hurricanes, including the titanic storm that all but destroyed Galveston in 1900. The old tower has also survived more than 75 years of neglect: its light deactivated by the Coast Guard in 1933, the tower was left unattended and has received only

minimal maintenance since that time. Now privately owned, the tower is still a familiar and welcoming sight to travelers, crossing the Bolivar Roads by ferry.

MATAGORDA ISLAND LIGHT
Matagorda Island, Texas

Its polished glass lens was hidden in the sand

In 1852, government contractors erected a tower on Matagorda Island, near Port O'Connor, much like the one completed that same year on Bolivar Point. The building was constructed in sections, made by bolting together heavy cast-iron plates. The 80-ft tower was topped by an all-metal lantern room, which was fitted with a third-order Fresnel lens.

During the Civil War, Confederate troops removed the expensive imported lens, hiding it, like buried pirate treasure, in a bank of sand. They believed, no doubt, that the lens would be retrieved after the Confederacy had secured its independence, which did not happen. The Confederates were less delicate when it came the tower itself, however; they tried to blow it up, using a charge of gunpowder, but the attempt failed.

Matagorda Island Light was built in 1852 as part of a chain of lighthouses constructed along the Texas coast. The original lighthouse, its tower identical to the one at Bolivar Point, was completed and placed in service in December 1852. The tower was rebuilt on the highest point of the island in 1873, almost two miles further inland from the original site.

OLD POINT ISABEL
LIGHTHOUSE

THE BEACON FOR THE COMMERCE
OF THE RIO GRANDE

ERECTED BY THE UNITED STATES
GOVERNMENT IN 1852

EXTINGUISHED DURING THE CIVIL WAR
DISCONTINUED, 1888 ··· 1895
PERMANENTLY DISCONTINUED, 1905

After the war, federal inspectors found the lighthouse still standing, but it was so badly damaged that it had to be pulled apart and reassembled from the ground up. Recovered from its sandy hideaway, the station's prismatic lens was returned to the lantern room and by 1873 was focusing the Matagorda Island beacon once again. Removed from the tower after the light was automated in 1977, the lens is now on display in a Port Lavaca museum. A modern optic now produces the station's flashing beacon, which can be seen out in the Gulf of Mexico for about 25 miles.

PORT ISABEL LIGHT
Port Isabel, Texas

Confederates won a battle here, when

they had already lost the Civil War

Built in 1852 to mark the approaches to the Rio Grande estuary, the Port Isabel Lighthouse stood on what was considered to be a strategic point, not only by sailors, but also at one time or another by the ground forces of Mexico, the United States, and the short-lived Confederacy. During the 1840s, General Zachary Taylor (later to be President Taylor) gathered his troops

here before embarking on his decisive invasion of Mexico. The lighthouse was used as a watchtower during the Civil War, and as an observation post by Union troops during the final battle of that fratricidal conflict. Known as the Battle of Palmito Ranch, the bloody, day-long struggle ironically ended in victory for the Confederates, who were as yet unaware that their side had already lost the war.

Its beacon returned to service after the war, the Point Isabel Lighthouse guided mariners until 1905, when it was permanently retired from service. The station buildings were subsequently put to many uses, and private or community celebrations were often held here. During recent years, the sturdy 57-ft brick tower has become the centerpiece of a local movement, aimed at revitalization and preservation.

In the 1800s, the low-lying Texas coast made charting a course extremely difficult, and it was clear that something must be done about it. The Port Isabel (Point Isabel) Light was constructed in 1852, near to the sites of the Civil War Battle of Palmito Ranch (1865) and the Mexican War Battles of Palo Alto and Resaca de la Palma.

VIRGINIA

K*nown for its green hills and blue mountains, its lush plantations and quaint country towns, its intimate association with the founding of the republic, and its Civil War history, Virginia is not widely regarded as a place closely linked with the sea. Virginians, however, are quick to point out that their commonwealth can claim one of the nation's oldest and most cherished nautical traditions. And it is the oldest, in fact, for the first Virginians braved the Atlantic before founding Jamestown in 1607, some 13 years before the pilgrims landed on Plymouth Rock. Many of the earliest Virginia planters were former seamen or maritime adventurers, who decided to settle down and try their luck ashore.*

The Virginia colony would never have survived at all, had it not been for its maritime trade with England and other European nations. Most of the weapons, tools, clothing, and other necessities it required, were imported by ship and exchanged for Virginia tobacco and produce. The Chesapeake inlets and river channels, that provided access to Jamestown, Williamsburg, and other early settlements, were unmarked and largely uncharted. As a result, more than a few trading ships came to grief on shoals, ending up as rotting hulks.

The competition between trading ship captains, based in American ports and in England, was one of the factors that led to the American Revolution. When the British blockaded Boston Harbor in 1774, Virginians were quick to join the struggle that led to independence. The Revolutionary War was won, and independence was secured, largely because a French fleet was able to keep British warships out of the Chesapeake, during the crucial Battle of Yorktown in 1781.

Virginia would become the birthplace of seven U.S. presidents, including the first, George Washington. Although never a seaman himself, Washington promoted and invested in maritime commerce. He was an enthusiastic proponent of maritime lights and, as president, encouraged construction of lighthouses in each of the former colonies. Not surprisingly, Virginia's first lighthouse, completed at Cape Henry in 1792, marked the highly strategic entrance to Chesapeake Bay. Over the following century, dozens of other lighthouses would be built to guide ships into Virginia ports on the James, York, Rappahannock, and Potomac rivers.

OLD CAPE HENRY LIGHT
Virginia Beach, Virginia

An early federal tower marked the strategic Chesapeake entrance

Few American structures are as historically important as Cape Henry's old octagonal stone tower. The building can trace its beginnings to 1774, when the colonial governments of Maryland and Virginia attempted to mark the strategic and commercially vital entrance to Chesapeake Bay. Tons of stone and other materials were assembled for the project, but the chaos of revolution soon called a halt. The project would not be revived until almost a decade after the last battle of the Revolutionary War ended in victory for the former colonists at nearby Yorktown.

One of the first tasks to be undertaken by the U.S. federal government, was the construction of the Cape Henry tower. Most of the materials stored at Cape Henry during the 1770s had vanished by the time construction recommenced in 1791, but by using freshly quarried sandstone, contractor John McComb had the 90-ft tower standing by late the following year. Although the project was

completed in a timely manner, it proved a very costly undertaking; Secretary of the Treasury, Alexander Hamilton, paid McComb, and other contractors, more than $24,077 to build the lighthouse, which was an enormous sum at the time, in that it was a significant percentage of the federal budget for an entire year.

But the government certainly got value for its money. In fact, the structure still stands, after more than two centuries of exposure to coastal downpours and buffeting by gale-force winds. Although its light was extinguished by the Confederates at the beginning of the Civil War, the lighthouse survived until 1881. That year a new Cape Henry tower was completed, and the light in the original structure was permanently extinguished. Although it has not functioned for more than 125 years, the 1792 tower still stands – now designated a National Historic Landmark.

NEW CAPE HENRY LIGHT
Virginia Beach, Virginia

Sheathed in a suit of armor

It it possible that mid-19th-century engineers were lacking in respect for the workmanship of their ancestors. During

the 1870s, when cracks began to appear in the walls of the original Cape Henry Lighthouse, government inspectors quickly concluded that the 80-year-old structure had to be replaced, and by 1881, a replacement tower had been completed. A 150-ft masonry structure, sheathed in a protective cocoon of metal plates, it was equipped with a first-order Fresnel lens. The huge prismatic lens remains in the tower and still focuses the station's beacon. Ironically, the original tower did not collapse, as had earlier been expected, with the result that Cape Henry is distinguished not by one but two historic light towers.

OLD POINT COMFORT LIGHT
Fort Monroe, Virginia

Confederate President Jefferson Davis was imprisoned here

No less historic than the tall Cape Henry towers is the relatively small lighthouse, located at Old Point Comfort, near Norfolk. Located on Fort Monroe, the octagonal sandstone tower rises only 58ft above the waters of the Chesapeake. But it is quite tall enough to have witnessed a broad swathe of American history in the making. Since

LEFT: The Old Cape Henry Light in the foreground, with the New Cape Henry behind.

BELOW: The New Cape Henry Light, completed in 1881.

VIRGINIA

ABOVE: The Old Point Comfort Light is the second oldest lighthouse on Chesapeake Bay. It was first lit in 1802, in the grounds of Fort George, which was the predecessor of the current Fort Monroe.

OPPOSITE LEFT: Its bold red-and-white stripes make the Assateague Island Light as efficient as a day marker as it is at night, when its powerful beacon is visible for 20 miles out at sea.

the tower was built in 1802, keepers standing in its lantern room would have watched British warships sail into the bay *en route* to their 1814 attack on Fort McHenry near Baltimore. Before the war was over, British troops were to seize Fort Monroe and use its lighthouse as a watchtower.

Old Point Comfort may also have witnessed the Confederate ironclad, *Virginia*, steaming out into the bay for its point-blank, canon-to-canon confrontation with the Union's *Monitor*, while at the end of the war, it may have seen the arrival of Confederate President Jefferson Davis, who was incarcerated in a cell not far away.

Fort Monroe is still a military base, and the Old Point Comfort Light is still

an active coastal beacon. The fourth-order Fresnel lens, placed here during the 1850s, remains in use, and the flashing red light it focuses can be seen from about 15 miles away.

ASSATEAGUE ISLAND LIGHT
Chincoteague, Virginia

Its red-and-white tower guards low-lying shores

Second only to the Cape Henry tower as a coastal marker, the Assateague Island Light is one of Virginia's – and America's – most important maritime beacons. Ships sailing along the Maryland and Virginia coasts, to the north of the

Virginia Capes and the Chesapeake entrance, are menaced by a maze of shoals. The low-lying shores in this border region, between land and sea, are difficult to see from the pilot house of a ship, and seamen need all the help they can get to avoid running aground. Since 1833, that assistance has been provided by the Assateague Island beacon.

The original tower was designed and constructed by Winslow Lewis, who had a hand in the establishment of so many early-19th-century light stations. The 142-ft red-and-white tower, seen here today, however, is not the one built by Lewis during the 1830s, but dates from 1867.

For nearly a century, the station's light has been focused by a first-order Fresnel lens. Since 1961, however, an airport-style optic now produces the beacon. The powerful Assateague Island light can be seen for 20 miles out at sea.

PORTSMOUTH LIGHTSHIP
Portsmouth, Virginia

A former floating lighthouse in an historic district

Retired from active service since 1960, the Portsmouth Lightship is now on permanent display. In 1986 it was set in

LIGHTHOUSES OF AMERICA

The Portsmouth Lightship can now be seen in the Portsmouth Naval Museum.

to shipping to mark with simple buoys, and too distant from the shore to mark with a mainland lighthouse beacon.

concrete on the shore in the Portsmouth Naval Museum. Visitors taking the time to tour the old vessel – once known to the Coast Guard as Lightship LV 101 – may realize the sort of dedication that was needed to keep a lightship and its beacon in constant operation. The crew's quarters, galley, workrooms and engine room, still look much as they did when the vessel marked the dangerous shoals off the coast of Virginia, Maryland, and several other eastern states. Like other lightships, this was used to guard obstacles that were too much of a threat

WASHINGTON

*F*ew states can claim a more intimate link with the sea than Washington, which was explored by George Vancouver and Robert Gray during the late 18th century, and by Meriwether Lewis and William Clark a few years later. The Lewis and Clark Expedition marked the beginning of America's westward expansion, and although the Columbia river was traveled extensively by the two explorers, it had in fact already been discovered by Captain Robert Gray in May 1792. Although Lewis and Clark arrived in the north-west by way of a cross-continental trek, the purpose of the expedition was essentially maritime: to find a navigable outlet to the Pacific Ocean. But the Columbia river, the mightiest river in the west, would not, as many believed at the time, become the north-west's most heavily trafficked maritime highway. Instead, most of the shipping turned toward San Francisco or into Washington's more northerly Puget Sound, with its torturous channels, numerous sheltered harbors, and access to Seattle.

During the mid 1800s, however, government leaders and maritime officials in Washington still believed the Columbia river would become the primary point of entry for western shipping, which is why they chose the banks of the Columbia as the site for one of the west's earliest and finest lighthouses. Erected atop the ominously-named Cape Disappointment cliffs in 1856, this light station played an unhappy role in the history of the west's early lighthouses.

Francis Gibbons, the builder of California's first lighthouses, brought his supply ship, Oriole, to the Columbia river in 1853, with the intention of completing the Cape Disappointment station that same year. But disaster struck instead, when the Oriole ran aground on a sand bar and was smashed to pieces by the surf. This calamity delayed the project for three years, dashing Gibbons's hopes of profiting from his ventures. Gibbons did, in fact, complete the lighthouse according to his government contract, which from the builder's point of view had been ungenerous to say the least.

Although building it all but bankrupted the unfortunate Gibbons, the Cape Disappointment Light has been guiding ships into the Columbia river for more than 150 years. Eventually, many other lighthouses would be built along Washington's outer Pacific coast, the Strait of Juan de Fuca, and the Puget Sound; many of these also have long and interesting histories, and more than a few are still in service.

CAPE DISAPPOINTMENT
Ilwaco, Washington

Marks the west's mightiest river

A generation after Lewis and Clark first saw the Pacific, near the mouth of the Columbia River, an 1848 federal survey designated Cape Disappointment as the site of one of the first lighthouses on the Pacific coast. The station was not established until well into the 1850s, however, largely because the supplies and materials needed for the project had been lost in a shipwreck in the Columbia estuary. Sufficient materials eventually arrived, and the lighthouse was completed and prepared for duty in 1856. It still guides ships today, more than 150 years after its light first went into commission.

The station's stone tower is only 53ft tall, but since it rests on the edge of a lofty cliff, its beacon shines out over the Pacific from an elevation of more than 220ft, making it possible for the light to reach vessels far out at sea. The beacon would have been even more effective, had the station's first-order Fresnel lens been left in place. Instead it was exchanged for a fourth-order lens in 1898, not long after the construction of the nearby North Head Lighthouse.

Alternating red and white flashes are seen every 15 seconds by seamen looking toward the cape at night.

NORTH HEAD LIGHT
Ilwaco, Washington

The windiest spot in America

The Cape Disappointment Light proved something of a disappointment to navigators, approaching the Columbia river from the north, where intervening cliffs made it difficult, if not impossible to see the light. To solve this problem, the government eventually ordered construction of a second lighthouse on nearby North Head. Completed in 1898, at a cost of $25,000, it was given a 65-ft tower and fitted with the first-order Fresnel lens that originally focused the Cape Disappointment beacon. Nowadays, a somewhat less powerful airport-style beacon produces the station's light signal.

As with Cape Disappointment, the North Head tower contributes only a fraction to the overall elevation of the beacon, but the cliff, on which it stands, places the light more than 200ft above the Pacific, making it possible for it to be seen more than two dozen miles out at sea.

WASHINGTON

Ferocious winds often whip across these headlands, some in excess of 150 miles per hour, and keepers have to take care to avoid being blown off the cliffs. This also applies to visitors, who arrive here from the Lewis and Clark Interpretive Center, at nearby Fort Canby State Park, to enjoy the extraordinary view and inspect the century-old lighthouse.

GRAYS HARBOR LIGHT
Westport, Washington

Washington's tallest light tower

Unlike the Cape Disappointment and North Head beacons, which gain most of their elevation from the cliffs on which they stand, Westport's Grays Harbor Light needed to have an unusually tall tower to enable it to reach vessels far out at sea. Among the tallest lighthouses on the west coast, the Grays Harbor tower stretches more than 100ft into the sky above the arrow-shaped estuary, that serves as an anchorage for the port of Aberdeen. Built in 1898, the octagonal brick structure has marked the harbor entrance for more than a century. The station's original third-order Fresnel optic had several bull's-eyes or focal points, that caused the light

to flash as the lens rotated. But the Coast Guard has since removed the historic lens, replacing it with an airport-style beacon. Visitors to the nearby Westport Maritime Museum will find exhibited there the giant first-order lens that once focused the beacon of Washington's Destruction Island Light.

POINT WILSON LIGHT
Port Townsend, Washington

Marking the entrance to the Puget Sound since 1879

Many of Washington's lighthouses do not face the Pacific, but rather turn toward the heavily trafficked ocean inlet, known as the Puget Sound. Reaching

more than 100 miles into the heart of the state, the sound only misses bisecting the wild and spectacular Olympic Peninsula by a few dozen miles, and

PAGE 239: Cape Disappointment is the oldest lighthouse in the state. The idea of siting a lighthouse on the cape was first mentioned in the 1848 act that created Oregon Territory, which included present-day Washington.

OPPOSITE LEFT: The North Head Light came into being because ships approaching the treacherous mouth of the Columbia river were unable to see the Cape Disappointment Light.

FAR LEFT: Gray's Harbor Light marks the best of Washington's few outer-coast harbors.

BELOW: The Point Wilson Light is the Puget Sound's welcoming beacon.

The Point Wilson Light marks the last leg of a difficult sea passage from the Pacific Ocean.

built, remains in use. In recent years, however, the lighthouse has become threatened by erosion; it may soon be necessary to move it, as has been the case with several historic lighthouses in the eastern states.

ADMIRALTY HEAD LIGHT
Coupeville, Whidbey Island, Washington

Once served as a kennel for military guard dogs

The beacon marking the entrance to Admiralty Inlet once shone from Admiralty Head on Whidbey Island. Established in 1860, it was a wood-frame building, its 41-ft tower standing on a bluff overlooking the inlet. The lighthouse, having been one of the earliest navigational markers in Washington and the west, served until the end of the 19th century, when it was demolished to make way for Spanish-American War fortifications.

In 1903 a new Admiralty Head Lighthouse was completed at Fort Casey, Coupeville. A Spanish-style structure, it consisted of a two-story keeper's residence with an attached tower. Only 30ft tall, the tower was quite modest in stature, but its location added

turning it into an island. Shipping channels in the sound are notoriously narrow and winding, and navigators must take care to avoid rocks and shoals. For more than a century, a chain of bright maritime lights have helped to guide vessels to safe harbors at Everett, Seattle, Tacoma, Olympia, and elsewhere along the sound. One of the foremost of the Puget Sound lighthouses is the one

at Point Wilson, near Townsend. Its beacon helps ships to steer a straight course into Admiralty Inlet, which links the sound to the Strait of Juan de Fuca.

Established in 1879, the station assisted vessels favoring the western entrance to the sound, and the lighthouse performs the same service today. The fourth-order Fresnel lens, placed here when the lighthouse was more than 100ft to its elevation, making its beacon visible from well out in the Strait of Juan de Fuca.

In 1922, the station was retired and handed over to the military for other uses. For a time it served as an army training facility for guard dogs, but in 1950, the historic building became the property of the state government and has since been restored. Nowadays, it serves as a museum and a popular attraction of Fort Casey State Park.

MUKILTEO LIGHT
Mukilteo, Washington

Brightens a former Indian campground

Passengers on Washington's Whidbey Island Ferry are invariably treated to an excellent view of one of the north-west's prettiest and most historic structures: the Mukilteo Lighthouse. The town of Mukilteo takes its name from a Native American word, meaning 'campground,' so it is likely that travelers have been passing this way for centuries, if not thousands of years.

Until about 100 years ago, however, those who arrived by water had no light to guide them, but this changed in 1906 when Mukilteo's lighthouse was completed. The station comprises a 30-ft

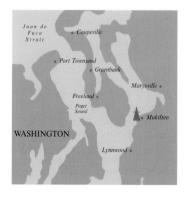

octagonal wooden tower, a fog-signal building, and a two-story Victorian-style keeper's residence. Although its size is unlikely to impress, the little Mukilteo Lighthouse has been guiding ferries and other vessels through the waters of Puget Sound for more than a century.

The Coast Guard originally planned to replace the station's original fourth-order Fresnel lens in 1960, but local preservationists banded together to block its transfer. The lens remains in the tower and still produces the bright Mukilteo beacon. The light flashes every few seconds and can be seen from a distance of about 14 miles, weather permitting.

POINT ROBINSON LIGHT
Tacoma, Washington

Began life as a foghorn

Fog enshrouds the Puget Sound so frequently, that foghorns are often more important here than fixed or flashing beacons. In fact, many of Washington's lighthouses began their active careers as fog-signal stations.

In 1885, for instance, the government placed such a station on Point Robinson, which projects dangerously into the sound just north of Tacoma.

Within a couple of years it was obvious that the point also needed a light, so a small lamp and lens were placed on top of the building housing the foghorn.

By 1915, the light was considered to be so essential to ships moving through the lower reaches of the sound, that a more conventional lighthouse was built. Consisting of a 38-ft concrete tower, with residences for a keeper and an assistant, the station was assigned a fifth-order Fresnel lens. The same lens still focuses the flashing Point Robinson Light, which can be seen from a distance of about 14 miles.

The Point Robinson Light is located on the easternmost point of Maury Island, in the south-eastern Puget Sound. Seattle can be seen just across the water to the north.

WISCONSIN

*B*oth the history and economy of this large Midwestern state have been deeply influenced by its access to the Great Lakes. Milwaukee, Green Bay, and other industrial cities along Wisconsin's Lake Michigan shore, often make initial use of the lakes to ship their goods to markets either in the U.S. or abroad. The state's prodigious agricultural production also finds its way to market, in long lake freighters and sea-going vessels that reach Wisconsin via the St. Lawrence Seaway. In fact, the liquid highway of the lakes has helped to make Wisconsin one of America's most prosperous states. This would not have been possible without the maritime beacons that guide the big freighters and warn them away from shoals and other dangerous obstacles.

The lakeshores of Wisconsin are marked by two large concentrations of lighthouses, one marking Lake Michigan, the other Lake Superior. Scattered along several hundred miles of shoreline, from the port of Kenosha, near the Illinois border, south of Milwaukee, to Green Bay far to the north, the state's Lake Michigan lights are by far the most numerous and diverse. Wisconsin has few notable ports on Lake Superior compared with Lake Michigan, and most are served by maritime lights. Since the mid 19th century, small but busy harbors, like the one at Racine, have welcomed freighters with bright approach beacons. In Racine, the job of guiding ships into port has been handled, since the end of the Civil War, by the soaring Wind Point tower, while at Two Rivers, near Manitowoc, the Rawley Point Light performs this important task.

An especially interesting group of lighthouses guards the dagger-shaped peninsula that forms Wisconsin's Door County, and separates the eastern side of the broad inlet known as Green Bay. The northern end of the peninsula is essentially an island, since it is separated from the mainland by a deep-water canal, linking the lower reaches of Green Bay with the open waters of Lake Michigan. Both the entrance of the canal, and the rugged shores of the peninsula, are clearly defined by shore beacons. In fact, Door County probably has more lighthouses than any other county in the United States.

Wisconsin has only a few Lake Superior lighthouses, but they make up for in architectural and historical interest what they lack in number. Most are found in the Apostles Islands, so-called because the explorers who discovered them mistakenly believed there were 12 in the chain, when there are actually 13. Located about 60 miles to the east of Duluth, the islands obstruct the southerly route through Lake Superior, and have long been seen as a threat to shipping. As early as the 1850s, the government began to mark the Apostles with beacons to guide freighters safely around the islands, which in time amounted to half-a-dozen in all.

Several of the Apostles' historic lighthouses remain in operation, but the old towers now have an educational role to play as the main attraction of a popular national seashore. Visitors, who flock here during the summer months, are encouraged to dream of what life would have been like a century ago, isolated on one of these remote light stations.

RAWLEY POINT LIGHT
Two Rivers, Wisconsin

Its upper level resembles a fancifully-decorated cake

One of the most remarkable structures on the Great Lakes, or anywhere else for that matter, stands by the shore to the east of the small lakeside community of Two Rivers. The Rawley Point Lighthouse has been guiding freighters and other vessels along Wisconsin's Lake Michigan shore for more than a century. Two Rivers was never a major port, and most local freight is loaded at Manitowoc, a few miles to the south-west.

The lighthouse was sited here, not so much to guide vessels into harbor, but to warn them away from a dangerous shoal. The land forming Rawley Point does not stop at the water's edge, but continues for a considerable distance to the east below Lake Michigan. To mark the shoal, in which vessels can easily find themselves permanently stuck, the government established a beacon there in 1853. The light emanated from the roof of a modest wooden keeper's residence, although neither this, nor a later brick tower, would be tall enough to provide adequate warning.

The most popular attraction of Chicago's 1893 Columbian Exposition was a 110-ft steel skeleton lighthouse. After the fair, the tower was pulled apart, shipped to Wisconsin, and reassembled on Rawley Point, where it remains to this day as an active aid to navigation. The tower consists of a central metal cylinder, secured by eight, heavily-braced, metal legs. Built to impress visitors to the exposition, the three-level lantern and workroom complex, at the top of the tower, is almost absurdly decorative, described by some as resembling a wedding cake. Despite its appearance, this is a hardworking navigational facility; its exceptionally powerful aerobeacon is capable of reaching vessels up to 28 miles away, in fact, nearly halfway across Lake Michigan.

WIND POINT LIGHT
Racine, Wisconsin

This unique double beacon was once produced by a pair of Fresnel lenses

During the second half of the 19th century, as the economy of the Midwest burgeoned, it was not only the major ports, such as Milwaukee, that became crowded with freighters, but also the

LEFT & BELOW: The Rawley Point Light was originally built to impress visitors to Chicago's 1893 Columbian Exposition. The three-level lantern and workroom complex, at the top of the tower, is almost absurdly decorative, and could be said to resemble a wedding cake.

Wind Point Light's 118-ft tower is attached to the keeper's dwelling by a covered passageway, similar to other Great Lakes lights designed by Orlando M. Poe. Within the tower, its iron steps are individually anchored to the walls and supported by a central column.

smaller ones, like Manitowoc and Racine. To guide all this traffic, the government established beacons all along the Wisconsin shore. At Racine, a pair of pier lights were put in place to indicate the entrance channel. These lights were relatively weak, however, and did little to assist mariners approaching from the north, since their view was blocked by Wind Point.

During the 1870s, the Lighthouse Board decided that Racine needed a much more substantial navigational facility and work began on a 118-ft brick tower and keeper's residence, located on Wind Point. Completed in 1877, the station utilized two separate Fresnel lenses for many years. In a highly unusual arrangement, a powerful

third-order lens provided the primary light signal, while a smaller fifth-order lens was used to mark a shoal just outside the harbor. Both of these lenses are now gone, and an aerobeacon now produces the light, which is visible from distances of up to 28 miles.

STURGEON BAY SHIP CANAL LIGHT
Sturgeon Bay, Wisconsin

Marks the entrance of a strategic canal

The long, narrow Door Peninsula separates Green Bay from Lake Michigan, forcing ships entering the bay to take a substantial northward detour. During the 1880s, a private

company excavated a deep-water canal across the middle of the peninsula to provide freighters with a short cut, thereby saving time and money. The canal earned the approval of ship captains, who preferred to avoid as much of the rugged peninsula coast as possible; but it was never particularly profitable, largely because navigators could not easily find the entrance. In 1893, the federal government purchased the canal, and a few years later established a maritime beacon at its eastern end.

The tower completed here in 1899 was a unique experiment, but its failure meant that it was unlikely to be repeated elsewhere. A series of relatively lightweight latticework supports were used to hold a central metal cylinder in place. It was an elegant but impractical concept, since the panels acted like sails during storms, and the wind howling in off the lake rattled the structure with such violence, that lenses and other equipment were frequently damaged.

After four years of enduring these bone-rattling vibrations, the keeper must have been delighted to see the latticework panels removed. Soon afterwards, the tower was rebuilt in a manner resembling the steel-skeleton

structure at Rawley Point. The lighthouse proved satisfactory, and still marks the canal entrance, more than a century after it was completed in 1903. The station utilizes its original third-order Fresnel lens.

BAILEYS HARBOR REAR RANGE LIGHT
Baileys Harbor, Wisconsin

Once used as a country parsonage

To the north of Sturgeon Bay and the entrance to its strategic canal, the rugged coast of the Door Peninsula offers little shelter to ships and crews caught in a Lake Michigan storm. Over the years, however, many beleaguered vessels have sought refuge at Baileys Harbor, located about midway along Door County's south-eastern coast.

To guide vessels into port, the Lighthouse Board established a pair of beacons near the harbor entrance in 1870. Like many entrance beacons on the Great Lakes, these are range lights, located one behind the other. The front-range light was housed in a small building, not far from the water, while the rear-range light was displayed in the window of a steeple-like structure on the roof of the wooden keeper's residence,

FAR LEFT: Baileys Harbor Rear Range Light is about a mile inland from the front range light. It was once used as a parsonage by Lutheran pastors, but is now a private residence. These lights are virtually identical to the ones built at Presque Isle on Lake Huron round about the same time.

located a short distance inland. For a time, the residence was used as the parsonage of a local church.

Although the station's lantern has been dark for almost half a century, its original fifth-order Fresnel lens remains in place. Now privately-owned, the building is surrounded by a wildlife sanctuary.

CANA ISLAND LIGHT
Baileys Harbor, Wisconsin

A crumbling brick tower, sheathed in iron

Ships approaching Baileys Harbor, from any considerable distance out on Lake

Michigan, rely on the beacon of the Cana Island Lighthouse, located just

north of the town. Completed in 1870, the station's 86-ft yellow-brick tower was fitted with a third-order Fresnel lens that made its beacon visible for up to 19 miles away. The same lens remains in use today and is no less effective than it was when placed in service nearly 140 years ago.

The Cana Island tower, on the other hand, would possibly not have survived to the present day without the protective shell of iron plates with which it is now encased. The bricks used to build the tower turned out to be of inferior quality and, exposed to the summer rains and winter storms, soon began to crumble. The iron shell, that has been in place since the early 20th century, halted the deterioration and saved the structure.

OLD MICHIGAN ISLAND LIGHT
Apostle Islands, Wisconsin

Built on the wrong island, the tower has served mariners for decades

By the mid 1850s, the discovery of iron and copper ore in the upper Midwest, and the opening of the locks at Sault Ste. Marie, had turned Lake Superior into a commercially vital maritime

OPPOSITE LEFT: The Cana Island Light is a tapering white tower, encased in cast-iron plates and topped by a two-story lantern, reached by a spiral staircase with about a hundred steps. With a focal plane 75ft above the base of the tower, the light's third-order Fresnel lens can be seen for up to 19 miles out on Lake Michigan.

OPPOSITE RIGHT: The Old Michigan Island Light. For reasons that are still not clear, the lighthouse intended for Long Island, not far off the Wisconsin mainland, was built on Michigan Island instead. Aware that a mistake had been made, it was decided to leave well alone, and the Michigan Island station was eventually activated. Consisting of a conical stone tower, with attached cottage, it remained in operation until 1929.

LEFT: Previously, the region's lighthouses had been rather basic, with little in the way of added ornamentation. The Outer Island Light (see also overleaf) was designed by Orlando M. Poe, whose design for the lighthouse was unique, in that it was intended not only to be functional but also to include design elements usually seen on more important public buildings.

WISCONSIN

thoroughfare. Unfortunately, the waters of the mighty lake were not particularly safe for ships, and many freighters, heavily laden with ore, ended their days in its murky depths. More than a few vessels, taking the preferred southerly route through the lake, blundered into the cluster of small islands, known as the Apostles, with disastrous results.

Among the many tasks undertaken by the Lighthouse Board, which took charge of the U.S. system of maritime lights in 1852, was a substantial expansion of service in the Great Lakes. Over the years that followed, many new lighthouses would be built there, including several in the Apostles.

The first such lighthouse was built on Michigan Island, at the eastern side of the Apostles chain, although, oddly enough, it was placed there by mistake, and for reasons that are still not clear, the lighthouse intended for Long Island, not far off the Wisconsin mainland, was built on Michigan Island instead. Aware that a mistake had been made, it was decided to leave well alone, and the Michigan Island station was eventually activated. Consisting of a conical stone tower, with attached cottage, it remained in use until 1929.

OUTER ISLAND LIGHT
Apostle Islands, Wisconsin

Guides vessels safely around the Apostles

Most vessels taking the southerly route through Lake Superior chose to go around the Apostles, rather than thread their way through the risky winding passages between these rocky islands. Since 1874, navigators hoping to avoid the islands altogether have looked for the beacon shining from the Outer Island Lighthouse, and once they have spotted it on the landward horizon, they

can rest assured that the islands are well to the south and no longer a threat.

The station's 90-ft cylindrical tower is one of the tallest brick structures on Lake Superior. Like many of the lake's other light towers, this is attached to the keeper's residence, a feature that was all but a necessity for a light station likely to be struck at any time by deadly blizzards. Most of the people who come here now, however, are unconcerned about winter storms. They are usually summer visitors, intent on enjoying the Apostle Islands National Lakeshore and learning as much as possible about its historic lighthouses.

DEVILS ISLAND LIGHT
Apostle Islands, Wisconsin

Warns mariners away from devilish red rocks

Devils Island is a strange name to encounter in a decidedly cool island chain, itself named in honor of the biblical apostles. The island was given this name because of its distinctive red rocks, that thrust toward the lake like pitchforks. The island and its stony cliffs were of considerable danger to shipping may have added to its diabolical

reputation. To keep navigators from skewering their vessels on the Devils Island rocks, government maritime officials established a beacon here during the 1890s. A wooden tower, built in 1891, was found to be unequal to Lake Superior's weather, and in 1898 it was replaced by the existing metal structure. The station's third-order Fresnel lens remains in place, but the beacon is now produced by a modern optic located outside the lantern room.

RASBERRY ISLAND LIGHT
Apostle Islands, Wisconsin

Visitors can relive lighthouse history

Much closer to the mainland than other Apostle Islands light stations, the Raspberry Island Lighthouse is a favorite of summertime vacationers to the Apostle Islands National Lakeshore, where reenactments are staged that give visitors a glimpse into the daily lives of lighthouse keepers and their families a hundred years ago.

Established in 1863, the Raspberry Island beacon served until 1957. The two-story keeper's residence still stands, as does the square wooden tower that rises from the front of the building.

SAND ISLANDS LIGHT
Apostle Islands, Wisconsin

Brownstone lighthouse warns mariners to keep their distance

Located at the far western end of the Apostle Islands chain, Sand Island was a threat to eastbound vessels, cruising too close to the Wisconsin mainland. The Sand Island beacon, established in 1881, was intended to warn navigators in plenty of time so that they could steer a course further from land that would carry them safely around the Apostles.

This remote light station does the same job today, while serving as a summertime attraction of the Apostle Islands National Lakeshore. The 19th-century octagonal brownstone tower and its attached cottage still stand. Originally equipped with a fourth-order Fresnel lens, the station now employs an airport-style beacon, which has a modest range of only about seven miles.

GLOSSARY

BEACON

The guiding light of a lighthouse is sometimes called its beacon. Often, the terms beacon, light, or light signal are interchangeable.

BREAKWATER LIGHT

A breakwater light is a lighthouse or beacon placed at the end of a long stone or concrete pier. The breakwater is intended to break the force of the waves, that might otherwise dangerously agitate the waters of a harbor. Usually, the light marks the harbor entrance and warns vessels to avoid the breakwater.

BUREAU OF LIGHTHOUSES

The organization that maintained U.S. maritime lights from 1910 until the Coast Guard took charge in 1939 was called the Bureau of Lighthouses. It was headed by a commissioner.

ELEVATION

The elevation of a maritime beacon is the vertical distance between it and the surface of the water. Because of the curvature of the earth, the higher the elevation of the beacon, the more likely it is to be seen from a significant distance.

FIXED LIGHT

Some lighthouse signals are fixed, meaning that the light does not flash or blink, but shines constantly from dusk until dawn.

FLASHING LIGHT

To help mariners distinguish a lighthouse beacon from other lights along the coast, some are made to flash at regular intervals.

FRESNEL LENS

During the 1820s, a French scientist, named Augustin Fresnel, invented a lens that could focus light into a concentrated beam visible from distances of 20 miles or more. Made from hand-polished glass prisms, assembled in a metal frame, Fresnel lenses often weighed a ton or more and could cost a small fortune. Fresnel lenses ranged in size and power from the massive first-order lenses, about the size of a small car, down to sixth-order lenses, about the size of a five-gallon jug. A few Fresnel lenses remain in use today, but most have been removed and placed in museums.

GREAT LAKES LENS

Because the waters of the Great Lakes are relatively confined, its lighthouses required beacons that were less powerful than those marking the outer coasts. The most powerful Fresnel lenses used on the lakes were slightly larger than an ordinary third-order lens.

LANTERN ROOM

Usually circular or octagonal in shape, and enclosed by glass, the room at the top of a light tower is called the lantern room. The lantern rooms of active lighthouses contain a lamp and lens or some other optical device used to produce the beacon.

LIGHTHOUSE BOARD

For more than half a century, beginning in 1852, authority over the nation's maritime lights was vested in the Lighthouse Board, a panel of innovative scientists, engineers, and U.S. Navy and Army officers.

LIGHTHOUSE SERVICE

The administrators, keepers, and other workers who maintained America's maritime lights, before the Coast Guard took charge of them in 1939, are often referred to collectively as the U.S. Lighthouse Service. The organization, though never formally recognized as such, is said to have been founded after the passing of the Lighthouse Act in 1789. The U.S. Coast Guard has adopted the service's heritage as its own.

MODERN OPTIC

Various plastic or metal devices have been designed to take the place of Fresnel lenses, which can be very difficult and expensive to maintain. Modern optics are much cheaper and can be computer-controlled.

OPTIC

The oil, gas, or electric lamps that produce a lighthouse beacon, and the lens or other such device that focuses it, are collectively referred to as the optic.

Pier Light

Often arranged in pairs, pier lights are used to mark the entrance channel of a harbor. Many pier lights are to be found on the Great Lakes, where harbor approaches are likely to be narrow and relatively shallow.

SCREW-PILE LIGHT

The shallow waters of bays, such as Chesapeake, needed to be marked by lights positioned directly over threatening shoals and shallows. To make this possible, small towers and keepers' cottages were placed safely above the tides on iron legs, which were attached to piles that were screwed securely into the mud and sand at the bottom of the bay.

SKELETON TOWER

When high-quality cast iron and steel began to be produced in about the middle of the 19th century, it became possible to build light towers with an open framework of metal. Often called skeleton towers, they consisted of a central cylinder, held in place by eight or more braced iron legs. Towers of this type were practical in areas such as the Florida Keys, where they were likely to be pummeled by hurricanes, and since they had no solid walls, high winds could do little damage. Several skeleton towers, built in the open waters of the stormy Florida Straits, have lasted for more than a century.

INDEX